The Essence of Dubai : A Travel Preparation Guide

Alexander Becker

All rights reserved. No part of this publication may be reproduced, distributed, or transmitted in any form or by any means, including photocopying, recording, or other electronic or mechanical methods, without the prior written permission of the publisher, except in the case of brief quotations embodied in critical reviews and certain other noncommercial uses permitted by copyright law.

Copyright © (Alexander Becker) (2023).

The Essence of Dubai : A Travel Preparation Guide	**1**
Alexander Becker	**1**
INTRODUCTION	9
CHAPTER ONE	**15**
• Welcome to Dubai	15
•About Dubai	19
• Getting to Dubai	25
•Visa Requirements	27
CHAPTER TWO	**33**
Essential Information	33
• Weather and Climate	33
• Currency and Exchange	38
• Language and Communication	43
• Transportation in Dubai	47
•Safety Tips	52
CHAPTER THREE	**59**
Top Attractions	59
• Burj Khalifa	59
• The Dubai Mall	64
• Palm Jumeirah	68
•Jumeirah Beach	74
•Dubai Marina	79
• Dubai Creek	83
•Dubai Museum	88
•Sheikh Zayed Grand Mosque	94

•Dubai Opera	100
• Desert Safari	105
CHAPTER FOUR	**111**
Shopping in Dubai	111
• Souks and Traditional Markets	111
• Luxury Shopping Malls	116
• Dubai Duty-Free	119
•Gold Souk	124
•Spice Souk	128
• Dubai Shopping Festival	133
CHAPTER FIVE	**137**
Dining and Cuisine	137
• Local Emirati Cuisine	137
•International Cuisine	141
• Street Food	145
• Fine Dining	149
•Traditional Arabic	153
CHAPTER SIX	**159**
Accommodation Options	159
•Luxury Hotels and Resorts	159
•Budget-Friendly Hotels	163
•Apartments and Vacation Rentals	167
•Unique Accommodation Experiences	172
CHAPTER SEVEN	**177**
Cultural Experiences	177
•Dubai Opera House	177
•Dubai Art Galleries	181
•Heritage and Cultural Tours	186
•Traditional Arabic Music and Dance	190

•Al Fahidi Historic District	195
•Dubai Miracle Garden	201
•Dubai Global Village	207
•Dubai Frame	212

CHAPTER EIGHT — 217

Day Trips from Dubai	217
• Abu Dhabi	217
•Sharjah	221
• Al Ain	225
• Fujairah	229
• Hatta	234

CHAPTER NINE — 241

Outdoor Adventures	241
• Dubai Desert Conservation Reserve	241
•Diving and Snorkeling	246
•Skydiving	251
• Hot Air Ballooning	255
•Water Sports	261
•Dubai Parks and Resorts	266

CHAPTER TEN — 273

Events and Festivals	273
•Dubai Shopping Festival	273
• Dubai Food Festival	277
•Dubai International Film Festival	282
• Eid Al-Fitr and Eid Al-Adha	287
• Dubai World Cup	292
• New Year's Celebrations	296

CHAPTER ELEVEN — 301

Practical Tips and Resources	301

•Important Phone Numbers	301
• Internet and Communication	305
• Health and Safety	311
•Etiquette and Cultural Considerations	315
CHAPTER TWELVE	**321**
Conclusion	321

INTRODUCTION

Welcome to the enchanting city of Dubai, a dazzling oasis nestled on the southeastern coast of the Arabian Peninsula. Renowned for its opulence, innovation, and remarkable architectural wonders, Dubai has swiftly emerged as a global hub for tourism, business, and luxury living. With its breathtaking skyline, pristine beaches, world-class shopping, and vibrant cultural scene, this modern metropolis offers a truly unforgettable experience for every visitor. In this comprehensive Dubai travel guide, we will delve into the city's rich history, explore its iconic landmarks, delve into its vibrant culture, sample its delectable cuisine, and provide you with invaluable tips to make the most of your visit to this extraordinary destination.

Dubai's origins can be traced back to the early 18th century when it was a modest fishing village inhabited by Bedouin tribes. However, over the past few decades, Dubai has experienced a remarkable transformation, evolving into one of the most cosmopolitan and progressive cities in the world. Today, it stands as a testament to human ingenuity and ambition, where futuristic skyscrapers pierce the heavens, man-made islands shape the coastline, and groundbreaking innovations push the boundaries of possibility.

One of the city's most iconic landmarks is the Burj Khalifa, the tallest man-made structure on Earth, which dominates the skyline with its majestic presence. Rising at a staggering height of 828 meters, this architectural masterpiece offers visitors the opportunity to ascend to its observation deck and marvel at panoramic views of the city, the Arabian Gulf, and the surrounding desert.

Another mesmerizing attraction is the Palm Jumeirah, an artificial archipelago shaped like a palm tree and one of Dubai's most extraordinary engineering feats. This magnificent island is home to luxurious resorts, upscale residences, and an array of leisure and entertainment options. Visitors can indulge in world-class dining, unwind at pristine beaches, or embark on thrilling water activities such as jet skiing or parasailing.

Dubai is renowned for its extravagant shopping experiences, offering a diverse range of retail therapy options. From traditional souks to ultramodern malls, the city caters to every shopaholic's desire. The Dubai Mall, one of the largest shopping centers in the world, presents a vast array of international brands, boutique stores, and entertainment attractions. Adjacent to the mall, you'll find the mesmerizing Dubai Fountain, where a choreographed water and light show captivates spectators with its enchanting performances.

Beyond its impressive architecture and shopping extravaganza, Dubai boasts a vibrant cultural scene that showcases its rich heritage and diversity. The Dubai Museum, located in the historic Al Fahidi Fort, offers a captivating journey through the city's past, providing insight into its humble beginnings and rapid development. The district of Bastakiya, with its narrow alleyways and traditional wind towers, transports visitors to a bygone era, exuding an old-world charm that is a stark contrast to the city's modernity.

To experience the authentic Arabian ambiance, a visit to the traditional souks is a must. The Gold Souk, with its dazzling displays of gold and precious gemstones, is a paradise for jewelry enthusiasts. The Spice Souk, on the other hand, immerses visitors in a sensory delight, with its aromatic spices, herbs, and traditional fragrances.

Dubai's culinary landscape is a melting pot of flavors from around the world. The city boasts an impressive array of restaurants, ranging from Michelin-starred fine dining establishments to street food stalls. Emirati cuisine, deeply rooted in Arabian traditions, offers a delightful fusion of flavors, with dishes such as machbous (spiced rice with meat) and luqaimat (sweet dumplings) tantalizing taste buds. For those seeking international fare, Dubai is a paradise for food enthusiasts, offering a vast

CHAPTER ONE

• *Welcome to Dubai*

Welcome to Dubai, a city where dreams become a reality amidst a landscape of modern marvels and ancient traditions. Located in the United Arab Emirates (UAE), Dubai has emerged as a global hub for business, tourism, and luxury. This travel guide will take you on a journey through the vibrant streets, breathtaking architecture, and diverse cultural experiences that make Dubai a destination like no other.

History and Culture:

Dubai's rich history dates back centuries, with its roots as a small fishing village on the shores of the Arabian Gulf. Over time, it transformed into a prominent trading hub, benefiting from its strategic location between Europe, Asia, and Africa. Today, Dubai stands as a symbol of progress and innovation while keeping its heritage alive. The city's museums, such as the Dubai Museum and the Sheikh Mohammed Centre for Cultural

Understanding, offer glimpses into its past, traditions, and Bedouin way of life.

Unforgettable Landmarks:
Dubai is renowned for its architectural wonders that push the boundaries of engineering and design. The iconic Burj Khalifa, the world's tallest building, dominates the city's skyline and offers panoramic views from its observation decks. Close by, the Dubai Fountain enchants visitors with its mesmerizing water displays set to music. The Palm Jumeirah, an artificial archipelago shaped like a palm tree, showcases luxurious resorts and is a testament to Dubai's engineering ingenuity. For a glimpse of traditional Emirati architecture, a visit to the Al Fahidi Historic District with its wind towers and narrow alleyways is a must.

Extravagant Shopping:
Dubai is synonymous with luxury shopping, offering a plethora of retail experiences to suit every taste. The Dubai Mall, one of the world's largest shopping destinations, houses high-end fashion brands, exquisite jewelry stores, and a vast array of entertainment options. Adjacent to the mall lies the Souk Al Bahar, a modern interpretation of a traditional Arabian marketplace, where you can find unique handicrafts, spices, and textiles. For a

more authentic experience, visit the traditional souks of Deira, such as the Gold Souk and the Spice Souk, where you can haggle for gold, spices, and souvenirs.

Culinary Delights:
Dubai's dining scene is a melting pot of flavors from around the world. With a myriad of international restaurants, celebrity chef establishments, and street food markets, food enthusiasts will find themselves in gastronomic heaven. Indulge in Emirati cuisine, characterized by aromatic spices, tender grilled meats, and savory rice dishes. Don't miss trying the national dish, Machboos, a flavorful combination of rice, meat, and spices. For a true taste of Dubai, venture into the neighborhoods of Al Satwa or Al Quoz, where you can savor authentic dishes from various ethnic communities.

Adventure and Leisure:
Beyond its opulent cityscape, Dubai offers plenty of opportunities for outdoor adventures and leisure activities. Explore the vast Arabian Desert on a thrilling desert safari, where you can ride camels, go dune bashing, or try your hand at sandboarding. For water enthusiasts, Dubai's coastline provides an array of water sports, including jet skiing, parasailing, and deep-sea fishing. The city's

numerous parks, such as Dubai Creek Park and Zabeel Park, offer tranquil retreats for picnics, bike rides, or simply relaxing amidst lush greenery.

Family-Friendly Attractions:
Dubai caters to visitors of all ages, making it an ideal destination for families. Dubai Parks and Resorts is a sprawling entertainment complex that houses motiongate™ Dubai, Bollywood Parks™ Dubai, and LEGOLAND® Dubai, ensuring endless hours of fun and excitement for children and adults alike. The Dubai Aquarium and Underwater Zoo, located within the Dubai Mall, provide an immersive experience, allowing visitors to marvel at marine life up close. Another popular attraction is the Dubai Miracle Garden, a vast floral oasis where you can wander through stunning displays of vibrant flowers and whimsical sculptures.

Festivals and Events:
Dubai's calendar is filled with vibrant festivals and events that showcase its diverse cultural heritage. The Dubai Shopping Festival, held annually, offers unbeatable discounts, live performances, and dazzling fireworks displays. During Ramadan, experience the city's traditional customs and enjoy sumptuous Iftar meals at various venues. The Dubai International Film Festival and the Dubai

Jazz Festival attract renowned artists and performers from around the world, adding a touch of glamour and entertainment to the city's cultural scene.

Dubai is a city that captivates visitors with its extraordinary blend of modernity, luxury, and cultural authenticity. From awe-inspiring architecture to lavish shopping experiences, adrenaline-pumping adventures, and family-friendly attractions, Dubai offers something for everyone. Embrace the city's spirit of innovation and exploration as you immerse yourself in its vibrant tapestry of history, culture, and breathtaking landscapes. So pack your bags, embark on an unforgettable journey, and let Dubai's wonders unfold before your eyes. Welcome to Dubai, the jewel of the desert!

•*About Dubai*

Dubai, the gleaming jewel of the United Arab Emirates (UAE), is a vibrant and cosmopolitan city known for its stunning architecture, luxurious lifestyle, and limitless opportunities. With its blend of traditional Arabian charm and futuristic innovations, Dubai has become a top destination for travelers from around the world. This comprehensive travel guide will provide you with essential information and insights to make the most of your visit to Dubai.

Getting to Dubai:
Dubai is served by the award-winning Dubai International Airport (DXB), which is well-connected to major cities worldwide. Numerous airlines offer direct flights to Dubai, making it easily accessible. Once you arrive, the city's efficient public transportation system, including metro, buses, and taxis, will help you navigate the city conveniently.

Climate and Best Time to Visit:
Dubai experiences a desert climate with scorching summers and mild winters. The best time to visit is during the winter months, from November to March when the temperatures are pleasant, ranging from 20°C to 30°C (68°F to 86°F). This period also offers clear skies and less humidity, providing ideal conditions for outdoor activities.

Accommodation Options:
Dubai offers a wide range of accommodation options to suit various budgets and preferences.

From luxurious 5-star hotels and resorts to budget-friendly hotels and serviced apartments, you'll find something for every taste. The most popular areas to stay in Dubai include Downtown Dubai, Jumeirah Beach Residence (JBR), and Dubai Marina.

Must-Visit Attractions:

4.1 Burj Khalifa:
No visit to Dubai is complete without experiencing the iconic Burj Khalifa, the tallest building in the world. Soaring at a height of 828 meters (2,717 feet), the Burj Khalifa offers breathtaking views of the city skyline from its observation decks. Be sure to book your tickets in advance to avoid long queues.

4.2 The Dubai Mall:
Adjacent to the Burj Khalifa is The Dubai Mall, one of the largest shopping malls globally, with over 1,200 retail outlets. Apart from shopping, the mall features various entertainment options, including an aquarium, an ice rink, a VR park, and a range of dining options to satisfy every palate.

4.3 Palm Jumeirah:
A man-made island shaped like a palm tree, Palm Jumeirah is an architectural marvel and a

must-visit destination. It is home to luxurious resorts, including the iconic Atlantis, The Palm. Enjoy pristine beaches, water sports, and indulge in world-class dining experiences on this palm-shaped island.

4.4 Dubai Marina:
Dubai Marina is a vibrant waterfront district known for its stunning skyscrapers, bustling promenade, and lively nightlife. Take a leisurely walk along the marina, hop on a traditional dhow cruise, or dine at one of the many waterfront restaurants overlooking the stunning yachts and sailboats.

4.5 Old Dubai:
For a glimpse into Dubai's rich heritage and culture, head to Old Dubai. Explore the historic Al Fahidi neighborhood, home to the Dubai Museum, housed in the 18th-century Al Fahidi Fort. Take an abra (traditional boat) ride across Dubai Creek to the bustling souks of Deira, known for gold, spices, and textiles.

Exquisite Dining Experiences:
Dubai is a food lover's paradise, offering a diverse range of culinary delights from around the world. Indulge in the finest international cuisines at award-winning restaurants helmed by

world-renowned chefs. Additionally, don't miss the opportunity to savor traditional Emirati cuisine and experience the flavors of the Arabian Gulf.

Shopping Extravaganza:
Dubai is synonymous with luxury shopping and extravagant malls. From high-end fashion brands to traditional Arabian souvenirs, the city caters to all shoppers. Apart from The Dubai Mall, other popular shopping destinations include Mall of the Emirates, City Walk, and the traditional souks in Deira and Bur Dubai.

Outdoor Adventures:
Dubai offers a plethora of outdoor activities for adventure enthusiasts. Experience exhilarating desert safaris, where you can go dune bashing, camel riding, and witness a mesmerizing sunset over the golden sands. You can also try your hand at sandboarding or embark on a hot air balloon ride for a unique perspective of the desert landscape.

Family-Friendly Attractions:
Dubai is an ideal destination for family vacations, with numerous attractions that cater to children of all ages. Visit Dubai Parks and Resorts, an entertainment complex featuring Motiongate Dubai, Legoland Dubai, and Bollywood Parks

Dubai. The IMG Worlds of Adventure, an indoor theme park, is another popular choice for families.

Cultural Etiquette and Dress Code:
While Dubai is a cosmopolitan city, it is important to respect the local culture and traditions. Dress modestly, particularly when visiting religious sites and public areas. Public displays of affection should be avoided, and alcohol consumption is only permitted in licensed venues. Familiarize yourself with the local customs to ensure a respectful and enjoyable visit.

Dubai's blend of luxury, culture, and endless entertainment options make it an alluring destination for travelers worldwide. Whether you seek architectural marvels, thrilling adventures, or indulgent experiences, Dubai has it all. With its world-class infrastructure, warm hospitality, and a perfect mix of tradition and modernity, Dubai promises a memorable and unforgettable journey. So, pack your bags and embark on a journey to this mesmerizing city in the heart of the desert.

• Getting to Dubai

Dubai, the glamorous city nestled in the Arabian Desert, has emerged as a premier global destination, captivating travelers from all corners of the world. With its stunning skyline, luxurious resorts, vibrant culture, and exhilarating attractions, Dubai offers a unique blend of traditional Arabian charm and modern opulence. In this comprehensive travel guide, we will explore everything you need to know to make the most of your visit to Dubai, from planning your trip to experiencing the city's captivating wonders.

I. Planning Your Trip:

Visa Requirements: Before embarking on your journey to Dubai, ensure that you check the visa requirements based on your nationality. Visitors from many countries can obtain a visa on arrival or through an online application process.

Best Time to Visit: Dubai experiences a desert climate, characterized by scorching summers and mild winters. The ideal time to visit is during the winter months, from November to March, when the temperatures are pleasant for outdoor activities.

Duration of Stay: Dubai offers an abundance of attractions and experiences, so plan to spend at least 4-5 days to explore the city's highlights thoroughly.

Accommodation: Dubai boasts a wide range of accommodation options, from luxurious hotels and resorts to budget-friendly apartments. Consider staying in areas like Downtown Dubai, Jumeirah Beach, or Dubai Marina for easy access to major attractions.

II. Getting to Dubai:

By Air: Dubai International Airport (DXB) is one of the busiest airports globally, serving as a major hub for international flights. It is well-connected to cities around the world, with numerous airlines offering direct flights to Dubai. Additionally, Dubai World Central (DWC) serves as an alternate airport, mainly handling low-cost carriers and cargo.

By Land: Dubai shares borders with Oman and Saudi Arabia. If you are traveling from neighboring countries, you can consider crossing the border by car or bus. However, ensure that you have the necessary visas and check the current regulations for land border crossings.

III. Navigating the City:

Public Transportation: Dubai has a well-developed public transportation system, making it easy to navigate the city. The Dubai Metro, with its extensive network, is a convenient and efficient way to travel between major attractions. The city's buses and taxis are also readily available and offer reliable transportation options.

Renting a Car: If you prefer more flexibility and independence, renting a car in Dubai is a popular choice. The city has excellent road infrastructure, and driving is on the right-hand side. However, be mindful of the traffic and parking regulations, especially during peak hours.

•Visa Requirements

Dubai, the gleaming gem of the United Arab Emirates (UAE), is a vibrant city that attracts millions of visitors each year. From its towering skyscrapers and luxurious resorts to its pristine beaches and cultural heritage, Dubai offers a unique blend of modernity and tradition. If you're planning a visit to this magnificent city, it's essential to understand the visa requirements to ensure a smooth and hassle-free journey. In this comprehensive travel guide, we will explore the various types of visas, application processes, and important information related to visa requirements in Dubai.

Types of Visas in Dubai:
Dubai offers different types of visas depending on the purpose and duration of your visit. Here are the most common visa types:

a. Visit Visa (Tourist Visa):
The Visit Visa, also known as the Tourist Visa, is designed for individuals visiting Dubai for leisure, tourism, or visiting friends and family. It is typically valid for 30 days, with an option to extend for another 30 days. This visa is non-renewable.

b. Transit Visa:
If you have a layover in Dubai and plan to stay for a short duration (up to 96 hours), you may be eligible for a Transit Visa. This visa is provided by the airline or travel agency you booked your flight with and is free of charge.

c. Multiple-Entry Visa:
The Multiple-Entry Visa allows visitors to enter and exit Dubai multiple times within a specified period.

It is suitable for individuals who frequently travel to Dubai for business or personal reasons.

d. Student Visa:
Students enrolled in universities or educational institutions in Dubai can apply for a Student Visa. This visa is usually sponsored by the educational institution and requires specific documentation.

e. Employment Visa:
If you have secured a job offer in Dubai, your employer will sponsor your Employment Visa. The visa application process for employment purposes involves various steps and requirements, including a labor card and residence permit.

Visa Application Process:
a. Applying through an Airline or Travel Agency:
For most types of visas, including the Visit Visa, Transit Visa, and Multiple-Entry Visa, you can apply through an airline or travel agency. They will handle the application process on your behalf and guide you through the necessary requirements.

b. Online Application:
Dubai also offers an online visa application process through the General Directorate of Residency and Foreign Affairs (GDRFA) website or the official

UAE government portal. This method is convenient and allows you to apply for a visa from anywhere in the world. Ensure that you have all the required documents and information before starting the online application.

Visa Requirements:
While specific requirements may vary depending on the type of visa, here are the general documents and information typically needed for a Dubai visa application:

a. Passport: A valid passport with a minimum of six months' validity from the date of entry to Dubai.

b. Visa Application Form: Completed and signed visa application form, either online or through the airline or travel agency.

c. Photographs: Recent passport-sized photographs meeting the specified requirements.

d. Proof of Travel: Confirmed round-trip flight tickets or travel itinerary.

e. Accommodation Details: Proof of hotel reservation or accommodation arrangement during your stay in Dubai.

f. Financial Documents: Bank statements or other financial documents to demonstrate sufficient funds to cover your expenses in Dubai.

g. Travel Insurance: Comprehensive travel insurance with coverage for medical emergencies, trip cancellation, and personal liability.

h. Invitation Letter (if applicable): If you are visiting friends or family in Dubai, you may need an invitation letter from your host providing details of your visit and their sponsorship.

i. Additional Documentation: Depending on the visa type, you may need additional documentation such as a sponsor's letter, student enrollment proof, or employment contract.

Visa Extension and Renewal:
If you wish to extend your stay in Dubai beyond the initial visa duration, you must apply for a visa extension before your current visa expires. Visit visas can be extended for an additional 30 days, while other visa types may have specific guidelines for renewal or extension.

Important Points to Note:

a. Visa Processing Time: The processing time for visas in Dubai can vary, so it is advisable to apply well in advance of your planned travel dates.

b. Visa Fees: Each visa type has its associated fees, which vary depending on the duration and purpose of your visit. These fees are subject to change, so it is recommended to check the updated fee schedule before applying.

c. Visa Validity: Make sure to check the validity period of your visa before you travel to Dubai. Overstaying your visa can result in penalties, fines, or even legal consequences.

d. Entry Restrictions: It is crucial to stay updated on any entry restrictions, travel advisories, or special requirements imposed by the UAE government or your home country due to unforeseen circumstances such as pandemics or security concerns.

Understanding the visa requirements for Dubai is essential for a smooth and stress-free travel experience. This comprehensive travel guide has provided an overview of the different visa types, application processes, and important information related to visa requirements in Dubai. Remember to check the latest guidelines and regulations from official sources before planning your trip, as visa policies can change over time. With the right visa in hand, you can explore the wonders of Dubai, soak in its vibrant culture, and create unforgettable memories in this mesmerizing city.

CHAPTER TWO

Essential Information

• *Weather and Climate*

Dubai, the gleaming gem of the United Arab Emirates, is a destination renowned for its stunning architecture, luxurious resorts, and vibrant culture. As you plan your journey to this desert oasis, it is essential to understand the weather and climate in Dubai. The city's unique geographical location and arid desert environment contribute to its distinctive climate patterns, ensuring a memorable experience throughout the year. In this travel guide, we will explore the seasonal variations, average temperatures, precipitation levels, and tips to make the most of your Dubai adventure, no matter when you visit.

Geographical Location and Influences:
Situated on the Arabian Peninsula's southeastern coast, Dubai enjoys a prime location in the Arabian Gulf region. The city lies at a latitude of approximately 25 degrees north, between the Arabian Desert to the south and the Persian Gulf to the north. These geographical factors significantly influence the weather and climate experienced in Dubai.

Dubai's Arid Desert Climate:
Dubai is characterized by an arid desert climate, featuring scorching summers and mild winters. The city experiences two primary seasons: a hot and humid summer and a pleasant winter. However, Dubai's climate can be further divided into four distinct periods: winter (December to February), spring (March to May), summer (June to September), and autumn (October to November).

Winter Season (December to February):
Dubai's winter is a respite from the sweltering heat, making it the most favorable time to visit. Average daytime temperatures range from 20°C (68°F) to

25°C (77°F), while evenings can be cooler, averaging around 15°C (59°F). These mild temperatures offer a pleasant atmosphere for outdoor activities, exploring landmarks, and enjoying the city's famous beaches. Light clothing and a light jacket or sweater are recommended for this season.

Spring Season (March to May):
Spring in Dubai showcases a transition from the cooler winter months to the hotter summer period. Temperatures gradually rise, with daytime averages ranging from 25°C (77°F) to 35°C (95°F). Evenings remain mild and pleasant, providing an ideal time for outdoor exploration. It's advisable to wear lightweight and breathable clothing, as well as sun protection, to ensure comfort during outdoor excursions.

Summer Season (June to September):
Dubai's summer season is characterized by intense heat, high humidity, and minimal rainfall. Daytime temperatures soar to scorching heights, averaging between 35°C (95°F) and 45°C (113°F). However, due to the city's modern infrastructure and extensive air-conditioning, indoor areas and malls provide respite from the heat. If you plan to visit during this season, lightweight and loose-fitting

clothing made of breathable fabrics are essential, along with ample hydration and sun protection.

Autumn Season (October to November):
Autumn in Dubai is a transitional period, as temperatures gradually decrease from the scorching summer. Daytime temperatures range from 30°C (86°F) to 35°C (95°F), with evenings offering cooler temperatures, around 20°C (68°F). This season presents an excellent opportunity to enjoy outdoor activities and explore the city's attractions comfortably. It is recommended to pack lightweight clothing, but also carry a light jacket or sweater for cooler evenings.

Precipitation and Sandstorms:
Dubai experiences minimal rainfall throughout the year, with the majority occurring during the winter and spring seasons. Annual rainfall averages around 100mm, usually in the form of short-lived showers. Sandstorms, locally known as "shamal," can occasionally occur, primarily during the transitional periods between seasons. These natural phenomena bring gusty winds and reduced visibility, but they are generally short-lived and do not significantly impact travel plans.

Making the Most of Your Visit:

To make the most of your Dubai adventure, regardless of the season, consider the following tips:

a. Sun Protection: Dubai's climate demands adequate sun protection. Wear sunscreen, sunglasses, and a hat to shield yourself from the intense sunrays.

b. Hydration: Staying hydrated is crucial, especially during the hot summer months. Carry a water bottle and drink plenty of fluids throughout the day.

c. Time Management: Plan outdoor activities during the early morning or late afternoon to avoid the peak heat hours and make the most of milder temperatures.

d. Indoor Attractions: Explore Dubai's world-class indoor attractions, such as shopping malls, museums, aquariums, and indoor theme parks, to escape the heat and humidity.

e. Dress Code: Respect local customs and dress modestly when visiting public areas, religious sites, and during the holy month of Ramadan.

f. Check Local Weather Updates: Stay informed about the weather conditions during your visit by regularly checking local weather forecasts or using reliable weather applications.

Dubai's weather and climate offer a unique experience to visitors throughout the year. Whether you embrace the scorching summers, revel in the mild winters, or explore the city during the transitional seasons, Dubai's enchanting charm remains unwavering. By understanding the climatic patterns and adequately preparing for the prevailing conditions, you can embark on a remarkable journey through this mesmerizing Emirati destination. So, pack your bags and get ready to be captivated by the wonders of Dubai, where every season paints a different shade of beauty.

• *Currency and Exchange*

Dubai, the vibrant and cosmopolitan city in the United Arab Emirates (UAE), is a popular destination for travelers seeking luxury, adventure, and cultural experiences. As you plan your visit to this stunning city, it's crucial to understand the currency and exchange procedures to ensure a smooth and hassle-free trip. In this comprehensive Dubai travel guide, we will delve into the currency used, exchange options, exchange rates, and practical tips for handling your finances during your stay.

The Currency of Dubai:

The official currency of Dubai, as well as the wider UAE, is the UAE Dirham (AED). The Dirham is abbreviated as "Dhs" or "AED" and is further divided into fils. Notes are available in denominations of 5, 10, 20, 50, 100, 200, 500, and 1,000 Dirhams, while coins are issued in fils and come in denominations of 1, 5, 10, 25, and 50 fils.

Exchange Options:

When it comes to exchanging currency in Dubai, there are several options available to visitors:

a. Banks: Banks offer reliable and secure currency exchange services, and you can find branches conveniently located throughout the city. It is advisable to exchange larger amounts of money at once to minimize transaction fees.

b. Exchange Offices: Authorized exchange offices, known as exchange houses, can be found in shopping malls, airports, and commercial areas. These establishments often provide competitive rates and extended operating hours.

c. ATMs: Automated Teller Machines (ATMs) are widely available throughout Dubai, accepting international debit and credit cards. However, it is essential to check with your local bank about any additional fees or restrictions before using ATMs.

d. Hotels and Resorts: Many hotels and resorts provide currency exchange services, but the rates might not be as favorable as those offered by banks or exchange offices. It is recommended to exchange a small amount of money initially and seek other alternatives for larger transactions.

Exchange Rates and Fees:
Currency exchange rates in Dubai fluctuate daily and are influenced by various factors, including global economic conditions. Banks and exchange offices generally offer competitive rates, but it's essential to compare before making a transaction. Keep in mind that banks may charge a small commission or transaction fee for exchanging currency. Additionally, some ATMs might apply

withdrawal fees or dynamic currency conversion charges, so it is advisable to be aware of these potential costs.

Tips for Handling Finances:
To make your financial transactions in Dubai more convenient and secure, consider the following tips:

a. Inform Your Bank: Prior to your trip, inform your bank about your travel plans to avoid any potential issues with using your cards abroad. Ensure that your debit or credit cards are activated for international use and inquire about any associated fees.

b. Carry Sufficient Cash: While Dubai is a modern city with widespread card acceptance, it is wise to carry a reasonable amount of local currency for smaller establishments, taxis, and other situations where cash is preferred.

c. Be Cautious with Exchange Offices: If using exchange offices, verify that they are authorized by the UAE Central Bank to ensure fair rates and avoid counterfeit currency.

d. Stay Updated on Exchange Rates: Monitor the exchange rates before your trip and be aware of the current rates during your stay. This knowledge will help you make informed decisions and avoid potential scams or unfair practices.

e. Credit Cards and Payment Apps: Credit cards, as well as mobile payment apps like Apple Pay and Google Pay, are widely accepted in Dubai. They provide convenience and security for larger transactions.

f. Emergency Funds: Consider keeping some emergency cash or a backup credit card separate from your primary wallet in case of unforeseen circumstances.

Understanding the currency and exchange procedures is essential for a hassle-free trip to Dubai. With the UAE Dirham as the official currency, various exchange options available, and practical tips for handling finances, you can navigate the city's vibrant markets, indulge in culinary delights, and immerse yourself in the unique cultural experiences without any financial worries. Remember to plan ahead, compare exchange rates, and stay informed throughout your visit to make the most of your time in Dubai.

• *Language and Communication*

Dubai, known for its towering skyscrapers, luxurious lifestyle, and vibrant culture, has become a global hub for tourism and business. As a cosmopolitan city, Dubai boasts a rich multicultural environment where people from diverse backgrounds come together. Language and communication play a vital role in ensuring a smooth and enjoyable experience for travelers visiting this bustling metropolis. In this travel guide, we will explore the linguistic landscape of Dubai, highlighting the primary languages spoken, the role of English, essential phrases to know, and tips for effective communication in this vibrant city.

Languages Spoken in Dubai:
Dubai is a melting pot of cultures and nationalities, with residents hailing from over 200 countries. As a result, a wide array of languages can be heard on the streets of this vibrant city. However, the official language of Dubai and the United Arab Emirates (UAE) is Arabic. Modern Standard Arabic (MSA) is the formal version of the language used in official documents, education, and media. However, the

local dialect spoken in Dubai is a variant of Gulf Arabic, which may differ slightly from MSA.

Role of English in Dubai:
English is widely spoken and understood in Dubai, serving as a lingua franca for communication among the diverse expatriate community and visitors. Due to the large number of multinational corporations, English has become the language of business, and many public signs, menus, and official documents are available in both Arabic and English. Moreover, English is taught in schools, making it prevalent among the younger generation. Travelers will find that they can navigate the city comfortably using English as their primary mode of communication.

Essential Phrases:
While English is widely spoken, learning a few basic Arabic phrases can go a long way in showing respect for the local culture and enhancing the travel experience. Here are some essential phrases that can be useful during your stay in Dubai:

Hello: Marhaba
Thank you: Shukran
Yes: Na'am
No: La

Please: Min fadlak (to a male) / Min fadlik (to a female)
Excuse me: Law samaht
Where is...?: Ayna...?
How much does it cost?: Kam thamanuh?
Multicultural Environment:
Dubai's multicultural environment offers a unique opportunity to interact with people from all corners of the world. Beyond Arabic and English, you may encounter a multitude of other languages, including Hindi, Urdu, Malayalam, Tagalog, Bengali, and more. Engaging with locals in their native language, even with simple greetings or expressions, can foster connections and create memorable experiences.

Nonverbal Communication:
Nonverbal communication plays a significant role in Dubai's cultural context. Understanding and respecting local customs can enhance your interactions and help avoid misunderstandings. Here are a few nonverbal cues to keep in mind:

Handshakes: When meeting someone for the first time, a handshake is the customary greeting. However, it is important to note that in some conservative settings, particularly when meeting individuals of the opposite gender, a handshake may not be offered.

Modesty in Dress: Dubai is a city with a mix of conservative and modern values. While it is generally acceptable to wear Western-style clothing in most areas, modesty in dress is appreciated, especially when visiting religious sites or government buildings.

Respect for Ramadan: If you visit Dubai during the holy month of Ramadan, it is important to be mindful of local customs. Eating, drinking, and smoking in public during daylight hours is prohibited, and it is polite to refrain from these activities in public places.

Translation Services:
In cases where language barriers become a challenge, translation services can be a valuable resource. Dubai has numerous translation agencies and language service providers that can assist with document translation, interpretation, and other language-related services. These services can be particularly useful for business meetings, legal matters, or more complex language requirements.

In Dubai, language and communication play a crucial role in facilitating interactions and enhancing the travel experience. While Arabic is the official language, English serves as the primary language for business and tourism. Engaging with locals and understanding their cultural customs, even with basic Arabic phrases, can further enrich your journey. With a diverse and multicultural environment, Dubai offers a unique opportunity to connect with people from around the world. By embracing the linguistic diversity and respecting local customs, travelers can enjoy a truly immersive experience in this vibrant city.

- *Transportation in Dubai*

Dubai, the dazzling metropolis in the United Arab Emirates, is renowned for its iconic skyscrapers, luxurious lifestyle, and world-class infrastructure. When visiting this vibrant city, it is essential to have a good understanding of the transportation options available. With its efficient and modern transportation network, exploring Dubai is a breeze. This guide will provide a comprehensive overview of transportation in Dubai, including public transportation, taxis, rental cars, and other useful tips for getting around the city.

Public Transportation :

Dubai's public transportation system is well-developed, providing convenient and cost-effective options for locals and tourists alike. The backbone of public transportation in Dubai is the Dubai Metro, a state-of-the-art automated rail network. The metro is divided into two lines: the Red Line and the Green Line. The Red Line connects major attractions such as the Dubai Mall, Burj Khalifa, and Dubai Marina, while the Green Line covers areas like Deira and Dubai Creek. The metro operates from around 5:30 a.m. to midnight on weekdays and from 1 p.m. to midnight on Fridays.

Another important component of Dubai's public transportation system is the Dubai Tram, which runs along the city's popular areas like Jumeirah Beach Residence and Dubai Marina. The tram system seamlessly integrates with the metro, making it easier to travel between different parts of the city.

In addition to the metro and tram, Dubai also boasts an extensive bus network. The Dubai Bus service covers almost every part of the city, including residential areas, business districts, and tourist attractions. The buses are air-conditioned and equipped with modern facilities, ensuring a comfortable journey for passengers. The RTA (Roads and Transport Authority) operates the bus network, and passengers can use the Nol card, a prepaid smart card, to pay for their fares.

Taxis :

Taxis are a popular and readily available mode of transportation in Dubai. The city has a large fleet of well-maintained taxis that can be easily hailed on the street or booked through ride-hailing apps like Uber and Careem. Taxis in Dubai are metered, and the fare includes a starting fee, distance traveled, and waiting time. The taxi drivers are generally professional and knowledgeable about the city, making them a reliable option for getting around.

Dubai also offers luxury taxi services, such as the Dubai Airport Taxi and the Dubai Taxi Limo. These services provide a more upscale experience with high-end vehicles and professional chauffeurs. While they may be more expensive than regular taxis, they offer added comfort and convenience, especially for special occasions or airport transfers.

Rental Cars :

For those who prefer more flexibility and independence in their travel, renting a car in Dubai is a popular choice. The city has a well-maintained road network and a straightforward driving system, making it relatively easy to navigate. There are numerous car rental agencies located throughout Dubai, including international companies and local providers. Visitors must hold a valid international driving license or a driving license from select countries to rent a car in Dubai.

While driving in Dubai, it is important to adhere to traffic regulations, including speed limits and parking rules. Parking is widely available in the city, with designated parking areas and multi-level parking structures. However, during peak hours or in popular areas, finding parking may be challenging, so it is advisable to plan accordingly.

Other Transportation Options :

Dubai offers various other transportation options to cater to different needs. For those who enjoy a more leisurely experience, traditional abras (water taxis) operate along Dubai Creek, providing a unique way to explore the city's heritage areas.

Furthermore, Dubai's innovative transportation initiatives include the Dubai Ferry, which offers scenic rides along the coastline and stops at several prominent locations, including Dubai Marina and Palm Jumeirah.

Additionally, for those who want to explore the desert surroundings, there are desert safari tours that include transportation in 4x4 vehicles. These tours offer thrilling experiences, including dune bashing, camel riding, and traditional entertainment.

Tips for Getting Around :
To make the most of transportation in Dubai, here are some helpful tips:

Purchase a Nol card to conveniently pay for metro, tram, and bus rides.
Consider using ride-hailing apps for easy access to taxis.
Familiarize yourself with the metro and tram timings to plan your journeys effectively.
Use the RTA's Wojhati app or Google Maps for navigation and real-time public transportation information.
Check for any ongoing construction or events that may affect traffic and plan your routes accordingly.

If driving, ensure you have the necessary documents and follow traffic rules diligently.

Dubai's transportation system is a testament to its commitment to modernity and efficiency. The combination of a well-connected metro and tram network, extensive bus services, abundant taxis, and rental car options makes getting around the city convenient and hassle-free. Whether you prefer public transportation or private options, Dubai offers a range of choices to suit every traveler's needs. By utilizing these transportation modes and following the provided tips, visitors can explore Dubai's magnificent attractions, cultural gems, and stunning landscapes with ease.

•*Safety Tips*

Dubai, the vibrant and cosmopolitan city of the United Arab Emirates, is a popular destination for tourists from around the world. Boasting breathtaking architecture, luxurious hotels, and a wide range of entertainment options, Dubai offers an unforgettable travel experience. However, like any other travel destination, it is important to prioritize safety during your visit. This comprehensive Dubai travel guide provides essential safety tips to ensure a smooth and enjoyable journey, allowing you to explore Dubai's wonders with peace of mind.

Cultural Etiquette and Dress Code
Dubai has a rich cultural heritage deeply rooted in Islamic traditions. Respecting local customs and adhering to the dress code is essential to ensure a positive experience. Here are some key points to remember:
Modest attire: While Dubai is known for its modernity, it is advisable to dress modestly, especially when visiting religious sites or public areas. Avoid revealing clothing, and women should cover their shoulders and knees.
Respect Islamic traditions: During the holy month of Ramadan, refrain from eating, drinking, or smoking in public during daylight hours. It is also important to be respectful of prayer times and mosques.

Public displays of affection: Public displays of affection should be avoided, as they are considered inappropriate in the local culture.

Security Precautions (approx. 400 words)

Ensuring personal safety and the security of your belongings is crucial while exploring Dubai. Take the following precautions to safeguard yourself and your belongings:

Carry identification: Always carry a valid identification document, such as a passport, and keep a copy of it in a secure location.

Stay vigilant in crowded areas: Dubai is a bustling city with crowded tourist attractions. Beware of pickpockets and keep your valuables secure. Consider using a money belt or keeping your belongings in a front-facing bag.

Secure your accommodations: Choose reputable hotels and resorts that prioritize guest safety. Make use of in-room safes or hotel safety deposit boxes to store your valuables.

Use licensed transportation: When using taxis or ride-hailing services, ensure that they are licensed and metered. Avoid unmarked or unofficial taxis, as they may not adhere to safety regulations.

Be cautious with your documents: Avoid sharing your personal information or documents with strangers. If approached by someone claiming to be a police officer, ask for identification and consider verifying their credentials by contacting the local authorities.

Emergency contact numbers: Keep a list of important contact numbers, including the local police, embassy or consulate, and your hotel's emergency line.

Travel insurance: Prior to your trip, consider purchasing comprehensive travel insurance that covers medical emergencies, trip cancellation, and lost or stolen belongings.

Health and Medical Considerations
Maintaining good health while traveling is essential for an enjoyable trip. Here are some health-related safety tips for your visit to Dubai:
Stay hydrated: Dubai has a hot desert climate, so it is crucial to drink plenty of water to stay hydrated, especially during the summer months.

Sun protection: Protect yourself from the intense sun by wearing sunscreen, a hat, sunglasses, and lightweight, breathable clothing.

Follow food and water safety guidelines: To avoid gastrointestinal issues, consume bottled water, eat freshly cooked food, and avoid street food or unhygienic food stalls.

Medical facilities: Dubai has a well-developed healthcare system, with numerous hospitals and clinics. Familiarize yourself with the location of the nearest medical facility to your accommodation.

Medication and prescriptions: If you are on medication, ensure you have an ample supply for the duration of your trip. Carry a copy of your prescriptions and any necessary medical documents.

Travel vaccinations: Check with your healthcare provider to determine if any specific vaccinations are recommended prior to traveling to Dubai.

Traveling in the Desert

Exploring Dubai's mesmerizing desert landscapes is an exhilarating experience. However, it is essential to prioritize safety while venturing into the desert:

Book a reputable tour: When planning a desert excursion, opt for a licensed tour operator with experienced guides who prioritize safety.

Carry essential supplies: Take sufficient water, sunscreen, and protective clothing to shield yourself from the sun. Pack a fully charged mobile phone and a backup battery.

Inform others: Before setting out, inform your hotel staff or friends/family about your desert excursion plans, including the expected return time.

Follow the guide's instructions: Listen attentively to your tour guide and adhere to their instructions regarding safety guidelines and equipment usage, such as wearing seat belts in off-road vehicles.
Avoid solo desert trips: Exploring the desert alone is discouraged. Traveling in a group or with a knowledgeable guide ensures a safer and more enjoyable experience.

Dubai offers a myriad of attractions and experiences that captivate visitors from around the globe. By prioritizing safety and following the guidelines outlined in this Dubai travel guide, you can enjoy a memorable journey filled with remarkable sights and cultural encounters. Embrace the city's cultural etiquette, secure your belongings, and take necessary health precautions to ensure a hassle-free and safe exploration of Dubai. With proper planning and awareness, your trip to Dubai is sure to be a delightful adventure that leaves you with cherished memories for years to come.

CHAPTER THREE

Top Attractions

• *Burj Khalifa*

Dubai, the dazzling city in the United Arab Emirates, is renowned for its opulence, grandeur, and extraordinary architectural wonders. Among its many world-class attractions, the Burj Khalifa stands tall as the epitome of engineering excellence and a true symbol of Dubai's ambition. In this comprehensive Dubai travel guide, we delve into the marvels of the Burj Khalifa, exploring its fascinating history, captivating design, and the unparalleled experiences it offers to visitors.

A Brief Overview of Burj Khalifa:
Standing proudly at a staggering height of 828 meters, the Burj Khalifa is the tallest building in the world. Its awe-inspiring silhouette dominates Dubai's skyline, offering a majestic backdrop to the

city's modern landscape. The construction of this architectural marvel began in 2004 and was completed in 2010. Designed by the renowned architectural firm Skidmore, Owings & Merrill, the Burj Khalifa is a testament to human ingenuity and a bold representation of Dubai's determination to push boundaries.

Architectural Marvels:

a. Unique Design: The Burj Khalifa's design draws inspiration from traditional Islamic architecture, featuring a sleek and modern interpretation. Its spire-like structure evokes the shape of a desert flower, with three wings extending from its central core. The exterior is adorned with reflective glass panels, providing stunning views of the cityscape.

b. Structural Engineering: The Burj Khalifa's engineering feats are truly remarkable. Its innovative design incorporates a bundled tube system, comprising of a reinforced concrete core and a perimeter structure of steel and glass. These elements work together to provide stability, flexibility, and resistance to high winds and seismic activity.

Observation Decks:

The Burj Khalifa offers two observation decks that allow visitors to admire panoramic views of Dubai and beyond.

a. At the Top, Burj Khalifa: Located on the 124th floor, this observation deck offers breathtaking vistas of the city, the vast Arabian Gulf, and the surrounding desert. Advanced telescopes provide a closer look at prominent landmarks and points of interest.

b. At the Top Sky, Burj Khalifa: Situated on the 148th floor, this exclusive observation deck provides a luxurious and intimate experience. With its stunning views and personalized services, it offers an unparalleled way to appreciate Dubai's splendor.

The Sky's the Limit: Unforgettable Experiences at Burj Khalifa:

a. Dining at World-Class Restaurants: The Burj Khalifa is home to several world-class restaurants, where visitors can savor delectable cuisine while enjoying breathtaking views. From gourmet delights at Atmosphere, the highest restaurant in the world, to a delightful culinary journey at The Lounge, every dining experience here is unforgettable.

b. The Dubai Fountain: Adjacent to the Burj Khalifa, the Dubai Fountain is a captivating spectacle of water, music, and light. With choreographed performances set against the backdrop of the Burj Khalifa, the fountain's displays are a sight to behold, creating an enchanting ambiance.

c. The Burj Club: Located on the 5th floor, the Burj Club offers an array of wellness and leisure facilities. Visitors can indulge in rejuvenating spa treatments, work out at state-of-the-art fitness centers, or relax by the exquisite rooftop pool, all while enjoying stunning views of the city.

Burj Khalifa: Beyond the Building:
a. The Dubai Mall: Adjacent to the Burj Khalifa, The Dubai Mall is a shopper's paradise and one of the world's largest retail destinations. It offers an unrivaled shopping experience, housing a plethora of luxury brands, entertainment options, and culinary delights.

b. The Dubai Opera: Situated near the Burj Khalifa, the Dubai Opera is a cultural hub that hosts a diverse range of performances, including opera, ballet, theater, and concerts. Visitors can immerse themselves in the vibrant arts and cultural scene of Dubai.

Tips for Visiting Burj Khalifa:
a. Pre-Book Tickets: Due to its immense popularity, it is advisable to book tickets for the Burj Khalifa in advance to secure your preferred time slot.

b. Choose the Right Time: Consider visiting during sunset or nighttime to witness Dubai's glittering skyline and the magical display of lights at the Dubai Fountain.

c. Dress Code: While there isn't a strict dress code, it is recommended to dress modestly out of respect for local customs and traditions.

The Burj Khalifa stands as a testament to Dubai's audacious spirit and relentless pursuit of excellence. From its extraordinary architectural design to its breathtaking views and unforgettable experiences, this iconic landmark has become an essential part of any Dubai travel itinerary. Visiting the Burj Khalifa is not only an opportunity to admire the world's tallest building but also a chance to witness the vibrant and ambitious city of Dubai in all its glory. So, make sure to include the Burj Khalifa in your travel plans and prepare to be captivated by its magnificence and the wonders it offers.

• ***The Dubai Mall***

Dubai, known for its extravagant architecture, luxurious lifestyle, and vibrant culture, offers a myriad of attractions to its visitors. Among these, The Dubai Mall stands out as a true gem, captivating tourists and locals alike. As the largest mall in the world, this retail haven offers much more than just shopping, boasting an array of entertainment, dining, and leisure options. In this comprehensive Dubai travel guide, we delve into the magnificent realm of The Dubai Mall, exploring its highlights, attractions, and the unforgettable experiences it offers.

Unveiling the Extravagance:
The Dubai Mall, located at the heart of Downtown Dubai, is an architectural masterpiece that showcases the opulence and grandeur of the city. Sprawling over an astonishing 12 million square feet, the mall houses over 1,200 retail outlets,

making it a shopaholic's paradise. From international luxury brands to local boutiques, visitors can indulge in an unparalleled shopping experience and explore a wide range of products, including fashion, electronics, jewelry, and more.

Shop 'Til You Drop:
With its vast selection of stores, The Dubai Mall caters to all tastes and preferences. Fashion enthusiasts can find haute couture from renowned designers at Fashion Avenue, while tech-savvy individuals can browse the latest gadgets and electronics. For those seeking unique Middle Eastern flavors, the mall offers traditional souks, where one can purchase exquisite carpets, Arabian perfumes, spices, and intricate handicrafts.

Beyond Shopping: Unforgettable Experiences Await:
While shopping may be the primary attraction, The Dubai Mall goes above and beyond, offering an abundance of unforgettable experiences for visitors of all ages. Let's explore some of the highlights:

a. Dubai Aquarium & Underwater Zoo: Home to over 33,000 marine creatures, including sharks, rays, and countless species of fish, the Dubai Aquarium is a mesmerizing sight. Visitors can stroll through the 270-degree tunnel and experience the captivating underwater world up close. The Underwater Zoo provides additional opportunities to engage with various animals, making it a must-visit attraction for families.

b. VR Park: Experience the cutting edge of entertainment at the VR Park, where virtual reality takes center stage. With an extensive range of thrilling VR experiences, including virtual roller coasters, immersive games, and simulations, visitors can embark on unforgettable adventures and explore fantastical worlds.

c. Dubai Ice Rink: Beat the heat and glide across the ice at the Olympic-sized Dubai Ice Rink. Whether you're a seasoned skater or a beginner, this facility offers a fun-filled experience for everyone. From public skating sessions to figure skating lessons and ice hockey, the rink caters to all ice sports enthusiasts.

d. KidZania: Designed for young minds, KidZania is an interactive and educational theme park that allows children to role-play various professions. From being a doctor or firefighter to a chef or journalist, kids can immerse themselves in a world of imagination and gain valuable insights into different careers.

e. Dubai Fountain: As the centerpiece of Downtown Dubai, the Dubai Fountain mesmerizes spectators with its breathtaking water and light performances. Set against the backdrop of the iconic Burj Khalifa, the world's tallest building, the fountain's synchronized dances to music create a truly awe-inspiring spectacle.

Culinary Delights:
Amidst the excitement, The Dubai Mall offers an extensive range of dining options to satisfy every palate. From fast food chains to gourmet restaurants, visitors can savor cuisines from around the world. Whether you're in the mood for traditional Emirati dishes or international delicacies prepared by renowned chefs, the mall ensures a gastronomic journey like no other.

The Luxury of Hospitality:
The Dubai Mall extends its commitment to luxury and hospitality beyond its retail and entertainment offerings. The mall is home to some of Dubai's most prestigious hotels, offering luxurious accommodation and world-class amenities. Visitors seeking a truly indulgent experience can choose

from renowned properties like The Address Dubai Mall and The Palace Downtown, which provide direct access to the mall and breathtaking views of the city.

The Dubai Mall stands as a testament to Dubai's ambition and its commitment to delivering unforgettable experiences to its visitors. With its unrivaled shopping options, awe-inspiring attractions, and culinary delights, it has firmly established itself as one of the top attractions in Dubai. Whether you're a shopaholic, an adventure seeker, or a food lover, The Dubai Mall offers a realm of possibilities to indulge your senses and create memories that will last a lifetime. A visit to this remarkable destination is an essential part of any traveler's Dubai itinerary, and it is sure to leave you spellbound and longing to return.

• *Palm Jumeirah*

Dubai, the glittering gem of the United Arab Emirates, is renowned for its architectural marvels and luxurious lifestyle. Among the city's many iconic landmarks, Palm Jumeirah stands out as a masterpiece of human ingenuity and engineering. Shaped like a colossal palm tree stretching into the turquoise waters of the Arabian Gulf, this man-made island is not only an engineering feat but also a world-class tourist destination. In this comprehensive Dubai travel guide, we delve into the allure of Palm Jumeirah, exploring its attractions, activities, and the luxurious lifestyle it offers to visitors.

I. A Brief History and Engineering Marvel:
A. Inception and Vision:
Palm Jumeirah, the brainchild of His Highness Sheikh Mohammed bin Rashid Al Maktoum, the ruler of Dubai, was conceived as part of the larger Palm Islands project. The ambitious vision was to create an artificial archipelago that would expand Dubai's coastline and provide a wealth of opportunities for residential, commercial, and tourism development.

B. Construction and Engineering:

Land Reclamation: Palm Jumeirah required extensive land reclamation efforts, involving dredging millions of cubic meters of sand and rock

from the seafloor and forming the distinctive palm tree shape.
Breakwater: A crescent-shaped breakwater was constructed to protect the island from erosion and rough sea conditions.
Infrastructure: The island boasts a sophisticated infrastructure network, including roads, bridges, tunnels, and utility systems, to support its vibrant community and thriving tourism industry.

II. Iconic Landmarks and Attractions:
A. Atlantis, The Palm:

Overview: The crown jewel of Palm Jumeirah, Atlantis, The Palm is a luxury resort that offers an array of indulgent experiences, including lavish accommodations, exquisite dining options, a water park, an aquarium, and a vibrant nightlife.
Aquaventure Waterpark: Thrill-seekers can revel in adrenaline-pumping water slides, lazy rivers, and a stunning dolphin encounter program.
Lost Chambers Aquarium: Visitors can immerse themselves in a captivating underwater world, encountering marine creatures ranging from vibrant fish to graceful stingrays.

B. The Pointe:

Overview: Situated at the tip of Palm Jumeirah's trunk, The Pointe is a vibrant waterfront destination featuring retail outlets, upscale dining establishments, and a picturesque promenade.
Dining and Entertainment: From international cuisine to fine dining, The Pointe offers a myriad of gastronomic experiences. Visitors can also enjoy live music performances and breathtaking firework displays against the backdrop of the Dubai skyline.

C. Palm Jumeirah Beach:

Pristine Coastline: Palm Jumeirah boasts stunning sandy beaches that stretch along its fronds, providing the perfect spot for sunbathing, water sports, and relaxation.
Beach Clubs: Exclusive beach clubs such as Club Vista Mare and Nikki Beach offer luxurious amenities, including infinity pools, beachside loungers, and delectable cuisine.

III. Luxurious Living and Hospitality:

A. Residential Villas and Apartments:

High-End Properties: Palm Jumeirah showcases an opulent collection of residential villas and apartments that cater to discerning buyers seeking a lavish lifestyle and unparalleled ocean views.

Signature Developments: Prestigious projects like One Palm and The Royal Atlantis Residences exemplify the epitome of luxury living, offering world-class amenities and personalized services.

B. Luxury Hotels and Resorts:

Diverse Accommodation: Palm Jumeirah is home to a plethora of internationally renowned luxury hotels and resorts, including Jumeirah Zabeel Saray, Waldorf Astoria Dubai Palm Jumeirah, and Anantara The Palm Dubai Resort.

Exceptional Experiences: Guests can indulge in spa treatments, fine dining, private beach access, and breathtaking panoramic views, all within the confines of these extravagant establishments.

IV. Activities and Experiences:

A. Yacht Cruises: Embarking on a yacht cruise around Palm Jumeirah allows visitors to admire the island's iconic silhouette and witness the grandeur of Dubai's skyline from the sea.

B. Skydiving: Adventurous souls can take the leap and experience the exhilaration of skydiving, descending from the skies to witness the stunning panorama of Palm Jumeirah.

C. Helicopter Tours: Helicopter tours provide a bird's-eye view of the Palm Jumeirah, offering a unique perspective on its palm-shaped layout and breathtaking architectural wonders.

V. Dining and Culinary Delights:

A. Culinary Diversity: Palm Jumeirah showcases an extraordinary range of dining options, from celebrity chef restaurants to traditional Emirati cuisine and international flavors.

B. Al Fresco Dining: Many restaurants on the island offer al fresco dining experiences with stunning ocean views, immersing guests in a world of culinary delights.

Palm Jumeirah stands tall as a symbol of Dubai's grandeur and ambition. From its groundbreaking engineering marvel to its opulent resorts, stunning attractions, and luxurious lifestyle, this man-made island has become a top attraction in Dubai. Palm Jumeirah offers visitors an opportunity to experience the pinnacle of hospitality, soak in pristine beaches, indulge in world-class dining, and partake in unforgettable adventures. As you plan your Dubai itinerary, make sure to reserve ample time to explore this majestic oasis and immerse yourself in the unparalleled beauty and grandeur of Palm Jumeirah.

•*Jumeirah Beach*

Dubai, the crown jewel of the United Arab Emirates, is renowned for its opulence, architectural marvels, and unparalleled extravagance. At the heart of this vibrant city lies Jumeirah Beach, an iconic stretch of sun-kissed shoreline that epitomizes luxury and leisure. This sprawling coastline, lapped by the crystal-clear waters of the Arabian Gulf, has become one of Dubai's most popular attractions, captivating tourists from around the globe. In this comprehensive travel guide, we will delve into the mesmerizing beauty, recreational opportunities, and world-class amenities that make Jumeirah Beach a must-visit destination for travelers seeking a perfect blend of relaxation and adventure.

History and Location

Jumeirah Beach, named after the affluent Jumeirah district it encompasses, has a rich history deeply intertwined with Dubai's evolution. What was once a quiet fishing village has now transformed into a thriving cosmopolitan city, and Jumeirah Beach has witnessed this incredible metamorphosis. Situated along the stunning coast of the Arabian Gulf, the beach stretches for approximately 14 kilometers, extending from the iconic Burj Al Arab to the Palm Jumeirah, an artificial archipelago.

Natural Beauty and Pristine Waters

Jumeirah Beach is an oasis of natural beauty, with its pristine golden sands and azure waters inviting visitors to unwind and rejuvenate. The beach is meticulously maintained, providing a tranquil escape from the city's hustle and bustle. Visitors can bask in the warm sunshine, take leisurely strolls along the shoreline, or simply relax in one of the many beachfront loungers.

The waters of the Arabian Gulf are perfect for swimming, with their gentle waves and pleasant temperatures throughout the year. Lifeguards are stationed along the beach, ensuring the safety of all swimmers. For those seeking more adventurous water sports, Jumeirah Beach offers a myriad of options, including jet skiing, parasailing, banana boat rides, and flyboarding. Water sports enthusiasts of all skill levels will find something to suit their tastes and preferences.

Iconic Landmarks

Jumeirah Beach is dotted with iconic landmarks that contribute to its charm and allure. The most prominent among these is the Burj Al Arab, a symbol of Dubai's architectural prowess. Shaped like a billowing sail, this luxury hotel stands tall on an artificial island just off the coast. Visitors can admire its beauty from the beach or indulge in a lavish dining experience within its opulent interiors.

Another architectural marvel in close proximity to Jumeirah Beach is the Palm Jumeirah. This man-made island, shaped like a palm tree, is home to luxurious resorts, including the renowned Atlantis, The Palm. Visitors can access the island via the Palm Jumeirah Monorail and explore its pristine beaches, upscale shopping avenues, and world-class entertainment options.

Leisure and Entertainment

Jumeirah Beach offers an array of leisure and entertainment opportunities for visitors of all ages. The beach itself is perfect for a range of activities, from picnicking and beach volleyball to yoga sessions and sunset walks. Families can take advantage of the dedicated play areas and barbecue facilities, creating memorable moments against the backdrop of the Arabian Gulf.

One of the highlights of Jumeirah Beach is the Dubai Water Canal, an artificial canal that connects the Arabian Gulf to the Dubai Creek. This mesmerizing waterway is lined with beautifully landscaped promenades, cycling tracks, and a variety of dining options. Visitors can enjoy a leisurely cruise along the canal, taking in the stunning views of the city's skyline.

For those seeking retail therapy, the beachfront is lined with upscale shopping destinations. The Jumeirah Beach Residence (JBR) Walk is a bustling pedestrian boulevard that offers an eclectic mix of boutiques, cafes, restaurants, and street performances. The nearby Dubai Marina Mall provides a seamless blend of shopping, dining, and entertainment experiences, ensuring there is something for everyone.

Dining Experiences and Nightlife
Jumeirah Beach is a culinary haven, boasting an extensive range of dining options that cater to all tastes. Visitors can savor delectable international

cuisine at beachfront restaurants, relishing breathtaking views of the Arabian Gulf. Whether it's a romantic dinner under the stars, a vibrant brunch with friends, or a casual meal with the family, Jumeirah Beach offers a diverse range of gastronomic delights to suit every occasion.

As the sun sets, Jumeirah Beach comes alive with its vibrant nightlife scene. Beach clubs, lounges, and rooftop bars offer a perfect ambiance for socializing, enjoying live music, and sipping signature cocktails. Visitors can dance the night away or simply unwind while taking in the panoramic views of the city's illuminated skyline.

Jumeirah Beach epitomizes the essence of Dubai, seamlessly blending natural beauty, iconic landmarks, recreational activities, and world-class amenities. Whether you seek a tranquil escape, an adrenaline-pumping adventure, or an indulgent beachside experience, Jumeirah Beach offers it all. From the pristine sands to the sparkling waters, this enchanting destination captures the spirit of luxury and leisure that Dubai is famous for. Make sure to include Jumeirah Beach in your itinerary, and let it transport you to a world of unparalleled beauty and unforgettable experiences.

•Dubai Marina

Dubai, the crown jewel of the United Arab Emirates, is a city renowned for its remarkable blend of modernity and opulence. One of its most iconic attractions is the Dubai Marina, an awe-inspiring waterfront district that has become a symbol of Dubai's grandeur and prosperity. With its stunning skyline, luxurious yachts, exquisite dining options, and vibrant nightlife, Dubai Marina offers an unforgettable experience for both locals and tourists. In this comprehensive Dubai travel guide, we will delve into the enchanting world of Dubai Marina, exploring its fascinating attractions, activities, and its significance in the city's landscape.

Historical Background

Dubai Marina's history dates back to the early 21st century when the visionary leaders of Dubai conceived the idea of creating an artificial canal city along the Persian Gulf coast. Construction began in 2003 and was completed in 2008, transforming an empty stretch of desert into a vibrant and cosmopolitan district. The Dubai Marina project aimed to create a world-class waterfront community that would rival other global cities, offering an unparalleled lifestyle and entertainment experience.

Architectural Marvels

Dubai Marina's skyline stands as a testament to the city's architectural prowess. Towering skyscrapers like the iconic Marina Torch, Princess Tower, and Cayan Tower grace the skyline, showcasing breathtaking designs and engineering marvels. The region's largest man-made marina, Dubai Marina is a sight to behold, encompassing an area of 3 kilometers along the Persian Gulf shoreline.

Exciting Attractions

Dubai Marina offers a plethora of attractions that cater to various interests and preferences. Here are some highlights:

A. The Walk and The Beach: Spanning 1.7 kilometers, The Walk is a vibrant promenade lined with chic boutiques, trendy cafes, and stylish retail outlets. Adjacent to The Walk is The Beach, a pristine stretch of sand offering stunning views of the Persian Gulf. Visitors can relax, sunbathe, or indulge in water sports and beachside activities.

B. Dubai Marina Mall: A shopper's paradise, Dubai Marina Mall is a luxurious shopping destination with a vast array of international brands, exquisite dining options, and entertainment facilities. From high-end fashion boutiques to entertainment zones like the indoor trampoline park, this mall caters to all ages.

C. Dubai Marina Yacht Club: A haven for boating enthusiasts, the Dubai Marina Yacht Club offers a world-class marina facility and hosts various sailing events throughout the year. Visitors can rent a yacht or join a cruise to explore the coastline and witness Dubai's stunning skyline from the water.

D. Skydive Dubai: For adrenaline junkies seeking an unparalleled adventure, Skydive Dubai provides an opportunity to experience the breathtaking views of Dubai Marina and Palm Jumeirah from the sky. Whether tandem skydiving or taking a static line jump, this experience promises an unforgettable thrill.

E. Marina Beach: Nestled along the waterfront, Marina Beach is a pristine sandy oasis where visitors can unwind and soak up the sun. It offers a serene escape from the bustling city, providing a tranquil atmosphere for relaxation.

Culinary Delights

Dubai Marina is a gastronomic paradise, offering a diverse range of culinary experiences to tantalize the taste buds. From high-end fine dining restaurants to street food stalls, there is something to suit every palate. The area boasts a multicultural dining scene, with cuisines from around the world. Whether craving traditional Emirati delicacies, indulging in fresh seafood, or savoring international flavors, Dubai Marina has it all.

Vibrant Nightlife
Dubai Marina truly comes alive at night, offering a vibrant and electrifying nightlife experience. The district boasts a wide range of bars, lounges, and nightclubs that cater to all tastes. Visitors can enjoy live music, DJ performances, and stunning views of the city's illuminated skyline. The stylish and sophisticated ambiance of Dubai Marina's nightlife venues attracts party-goers from around the world.

Accommodation Options
Dubai Marina offers an array of accommodation options that cater to every budget and preference. Luxurious waterfront hotels and resorts provide opulent experiences with stunning views of the marina. Additionally, there are numerous serviced apartments and rental properties available, offering convenience and flexibility for longer stays.

Dubai Marina stands as a testament to Dubai's ambition, grandeur, and ability to transform dreams into reality. As a premier destination, it encapsulates the essence of Dubai's modernity, luxury, and vibrant lifestyle. From its architectural marvels to its exciting attractions, diverse dining options, and pulsating nightlife, Dubai Marina offers a complete sensory experience for visitors. Exploring the district's rich tapestry of experiences leaves an indelible impression on travelers, making Dubai Marina a must-visit destination in Dubai. Immerse yourself in the glamour and beauty of this enchanting waterfront district, and witness the magic that has made Dubai a global icon of luxury and modernity.

• *Dubai Creek*

Dubai, known as the "City of Gold," is a mesmerizing destination that seamlessly blends modern marvels with rich cultural heritage. One of the city's most iconic attractions is Dubai Creek, a historical waterway that has played a pivotal role in shaping the emirate's identity. This bustling waterfront, flanked by a vibrant blend of traditional and modern architecture, offers visitors a unique glimpse into Dubai's past and present. In this comprehensive Dubai travel guide, we will delve into the fascinating world of Dubai Creek, exploring its historical significance, top attractions, and cultural experiences that make it an absolute must-visit destination.

I. Historical Significance

Dubai Creek has long been the heart and soul of Dubai, serving as a vital trading route and a hub of economic activity for centuries. Its strategic location on the Arabian Gulf made it an ideal harbor, attracting merchants from across the globe. The creek's rich history dates back to the time when Dubai was a humble fishing and pearl diving village.

During the 19th century, Dubai Creek thrived as a bustling port, facilitating trade between India, Africa, and the Middle East. Traditional dhows, wooden sailing vessels, were a common sight, transporting goods such as spices, textiles, and pearls. Today, visitors can still witness the charm of these traditional boats as they sail along the creek, paying homage to Dubai's trading roots.

II. Top Attractions along Dubai Creek

The Dubai Creek Golf & Yacht Club: Located on the shores of Dubai Creek, this world-class golf and yacht club is a haven for sports enthusiasts. The club's iconic sail-shaped clubhouse, designed to resemble a traditional dhow, is an architectural masterpiece. Golfers can enjoy teeing off against a backdrop of stunning waterfront views, while the marina offers an opportunity to explore Dubai's coastline aboard luxury yachts.

Al Fahidi Historic District: Nestled along the Dubai Creek's southern bank, Al Fahidi is one of Dubai's oldest neighborhoods. Its narrow lanes are lined with traditional wind-tower houses, showcasing traditional Emirati architecture. The district also houses the Dubai Museum, offering a captivating journey through Dubai's past with exhibits on Bedouin life, pearl diving, and the city's transformation.

Gold and Spice Souks: A visit to Dubai Creek would be incomplete without exploring the vibrant souks. The Gold Souk is a treasure trove of shimmering jewelry, with countless stores offering exquisite gold, diamonds, and gemstones. Just a short stroll away is the Spice Souk, where the air is filled with aromatic scents of exotic spices, herbs, and fragrances.

Dubai Creek Park: Stretching across 96 hectares, Dubai Creek Park is a sprawling green oasis where visitors can escape the city's bustling energy. The park offers a range of recreational facilities, including jogging tracks, picnic areas, and children's play zones. Its prime location along the creek provides breathtaking views of the skyline and the passing dhows.

Dubai Creek Dhow Cruise: A dhow cruise along Dubai Creek is a quintessential Dubai experience. Visitors can board a traditional wooden dhow and embark on a relaxing journey, taking in the sights and sounds of the creek. The evening cruises are particularly enchanting, as the city lights illuminate the waterfront, creating a magical ambiance.

III. Cultural Experiences

Dubai Creek offers a wealth of cultural experiences that allow visitors to immerse themselves in Emirati traditions and customs.

Abras: Taking a traditional abra (water taxi) across Dubai Creek is an authentic way to experience the city's heritage. These small wooden boats ferry passengers from one side of the creek to the other, offering panoramic views of the bustling waterfront. The abras are not only a mode of transportation but also a cherished symbol of Dubai's past.

Traditional Emirati Cuisine: Along the creek's promenade, visitors can savor traditional Emirati cuisine at various restaurants and cafes. From aromatic Arabian coffee and freshly baked bread to delectable seafood and succulent meat dishes, the culinary offerings showcase the flavors of the region.

Heritage and Diving Village: Located near the mouth of the creek, the Heritage and Diving Village is a living museum that highlights the UAE's rich cultural heritage. Visitors can witness traditional crafts, watch pearl diving demonstrations, and explore the Bedouin encampments to gain insights into the nomadic way of life.

IV. Future Developments
Dubai Creek continues to evolve and transform as Dubai embraces the future while honoring its past. The Dubai Creek Harbor, an ambitious development project, aims to redefine waterfront living and create a vibrant community that

seamlessly integrates residential, commercial, and leisure spaces. The centerpiece of this project is the Dubai Creek Tower, set to become the tallest structure in the world upon its completion.

Dubai Creek stands as a testament to the city's remarkable journey from a humble trading port to a global metropolis. Its historical significance, combined with an array of top attractions and cultural experiences, makes it an integral part of any Dubai travel itinerary. A visit to Dubai Creek is not just about admiring stunning architecture and exploring vibrant souks, but also about immersing oneself in the city's rich heritage and embracing the warmth of Emirati traditions. So, embark on a captivating journey through time and culture, and let Dubai Creek leave an indelible mark on your travel memories.

•*Dubai Museum*

Dubai, the glittering jewel of the United Arab Emirates, is renowned for its modern skyscrapers, luxurious resorts, and extravagant lifestyle. Amidst the contemporary marvels, Dubai Museum stands as a timeless testament to the city's rich history and cultural heritage. Located in the historic Al Fahidi Fort, the museum offers visitors a captivating journey back in time, shedding light on Dubai's transformation from a modest fishing village to a global metropolis. This comprehensive Dubai travel guide will delve into the fascinating world of Dubai Museum, highlighting its top attractions, historical significance, and immersive experiences.

Historical Background:

Dubai Museum is housed within the Al Fahidi Fort, a stunning architectural masterpiece that dates back to the late 18th century. Originally built as a defense structure to guard Dubai Creek, the fort played a vital role in safeguarding the city from invasions. The fort's strategic location served as a pivotal point for the rulers of Dubai to control trade routes and protect their territories. In 1971, the fort was transformed into Dubai Museum with the vision of preserving the city's cultural heritage.

Architectural Marvel :

The Al Fahidi Fort's distinctive design reflects traditional Arabian architecture, with its thick walls constructed from coral blocks and gypsum plaster. The fort's towering watchtowers, wooden ceilings, and decorative wind towers (Barajeel) offer visitors a glimpse into the ingenious architectural techniques employed in the past to combat the harsh desert climate. The serene courtyard within the fort further enhances the historical ambiance, inviting visitors to explore the rich tapestry of Dubai's past.

Exhibitions and Galleries :

Dubai Museum boasts a plethora of exhibitions and galleries that offer a comprehensive insight into the city's history, culture, and traditions. The exhibits are thoughtfully curated and presented to engage visitors of all ages. Here are some of the prominent attractions within the museum:

a. Pearl Diving: Experience the ancient trade of pearl diving, which was once the backbone of Dubai's economy. The exhibit showcases original diving equipment, intricate pearl jewelry, and vivid narratives of the perilous diving expeditions.

b. Dubai Creek: Discover the pivotal role of Dubai Creek in the city's development as a hub of maritime trade. Lifelike dioramas and interactive displays depict the bustling port and its significance in connecting Dubai to the wider world.

c. Bedouin Life: Immerse yourself in the nomadic lifestyle of the Bedouin tribes that inhabited the region before Dubai's urbanization. The exhibit showcases traditional Bedouin tents, authentic artifacts, and informative displays on their customs and traditions.

d. Traditional Architecture: Explore the architectural evolution of Dubai through intricate models, photographs, and artifacts. Gain insights into the design principles that have shaped the city's iconic landmarks, such as wind towers, courtyard houses, and mosques.

e. Dubai's Transformation: Witness Dubai's meteoric rise from a modest fishing village to a global city of awe-inspiring architecture and opulence. This exhibit uses multimedia presentations, scale models, and historical photographs to depict the city's transformation.

f. Calligraphy and Arabesque: Appreciate the artistic mastery of Arabic calligraphy and the intricate beauty of Arabesque designs. Discover the cultural significance of these art forms and their integration into various aspects of Emirati life.

Interactive Experiences :

Dubai Museum goes beyond static displays, offering visitors a range of interactive experiences to make the journey even more engaging. These experiences include:

a. Cultural Performances: Delight in traditional Emirati dance and music performances that showcase the region's vibrant artistic heritage. From mesmerizing sword dances to rhythmic drumming, these performances transport visitors to a bygone era.

b. Traditional Souq: Step into a recreated traditional souq (market) within the museum, where visitors can witness the bustling atmosphere of a traditional Emirati market. Browse through stalls selling spices, textiles, handicrafts, and other traditional wares.

c. Virtual Reality: Experience Dubai's historical landmarks and heritage sites through cutting-edge virtual reality technology. Take a virtual tour of ancient Dubai, explore the Al Fahidi Fort in its original form, and immerse yourself in the vibrant history of the city.

Practical Information and Tips :

Location: Dubai Museum is located in the Al Fahidi neighborhood, near Dubai Creek in Bur Dubai.

Opening Hours: The museum is open from 8:30 AM to 8:30 PM from Saturday to Thursday, and from 2:30 PM to 8:30 PM on Fridays.

Entry Fees: The admission fee for adults is AED 3 (approximately USD 0.82), and AED 1 (approximately USD 0.27) for children under six years old.

Guided Tours: The museum offers informative guided tours in multiple languages, providing in-depth knowledge about the exhibits and the history of Dubai.

Photography: Visitors are allowed to take non-flash photographs in most areas of the museum, but restrictions may apply in certain sections.

Accessibility: The museum is wheelchair accessible, ensuring that visitors with mobility challenges can explore the exhibits comfortably.

Conclusion (150 words):

Dubai Museum stands as a testament to Dubai's deep-rooted heritage and its remarkable journey from a humble trading post to a global powerhouse. With its captivating exhibitions, immersive experiences, and stunning architectural design, the museum offers a captivating glimpse into Dubai's rich history and cultural traditions. A visit to Dubai Museum is an essential part of any traveler's itinerary, as it provides a unique perspective on the city's transformation and allows visitors to appreciate the proud heritage of the Emirati people. By exploring the museum's exhibits, engaging in interactive experiences, and delving into the city's past, visitors can gain a deeper understanding and appreciation of Dubai's present-day marvels.

•*Sheikh Zayed Grand Mosque*

Dubai, the glittering gem of the United Arab Emirates, boasts an array of remarkable attractions that captivate the hearts of travelers from around the world. Among these treasures lies the Sheikh Zayed Grand Mosque, an architectural masterpiece that stands as a testament to Dubai's grandeur and cultural heritage. With its awe-inspiring design, intricate craftsmanship, and profound religious significance, the mosque has become an iconic symbol of Dubai's rich history and contemporary allure. In this comprehensive Dubai travel guide, we delve into the captivating allure of the Sheikh Zayed Grand Mosque, exploring its history, architecture, cultural significance, and practical tips for visitors.

History and Significance
The Sheikh Zayed Grand Mosque was commissioned by the late Sheikh Zayed bin Sultan Al Nahyan, the founder and first President of the United Arab Emirates. His vision was to create a place of worship that would embrace the cultural diversity of the UAE and serve as a symbol of peace, unity, and religious tolerance. Construction began in 1996 and was completed in 2007, culminating in a stunning architectural marvel that now attracts millions of visitors each year.

The mosque holds significant historical and cultural value for the UAE. It is named after Sheikh Zayed, who is revered as the Father of the Nation for his visionary leadership and contributions to the country's development. The mosque's design incorporates elements from various Islamic architectural styles, showcasing the rich heritage of the Islamic world and honoring the values cherished by Sheikh Zayed.

Architectural Marvel
The Sheikh Zayed Grand Mosque is a testament to architectural brilliance, combining traditional

Islamic designs with modern techniques. The mosque's design draws inspiration from Persian, Mughal, and Moorish architectural styles, resulting in a breathtaking fusion of artistic motifs and geometric patterns.

The mosque covers an expansive area of over 30 acres and can accommodate up to 40,000 worshippers at a time. Its exterior features exquisite white marble panels adorned with intricate floral designs, complemented by decorative calligraphy in various verses from the Quran. The iconic 82 domes, each clad in white marble and adorned with gold-gilded finials, add a touch of majesty to the structure.

Upon entering the mosque, visitors are greeted by the stunning main prayer hall, adorned with one of the world's largest chandeliers, weighing over 12 tons and featuring thousands of Swarovski crystals. The Persian carpets, crafted by skilled artisans, cover the vast expanse of the prayer hall, showcasing intricate patterns and designs. The mosque also houses the world's largest hand-knotted carpet, measuring over 60,000 square feet and weighing 35 tons.

Cultural Significance and Religious Practices

Beyond its architectural magnificence, the Sheikh Zayed Grand Mosque holds profound cultural and religious significance for both locals and visitors. As one of the few mosques in the UAE open to non-Muslims, it provides a unique opportunity to learn about Islamic traditions, customs, and practices.

Visitors are encouraged to respect the mosque's religious sanctity by adhering to the dress code, which requires modest attire for both men and women. Traditional abayas and kanduras are available for loan at the entrance, allowing all visitors to comply with the guidelines. Shoes must be removed before entering the mosque, and separate prayer areas are designated for men and women.

Throughout the year, the mosque hosts various educational and cultural programs that promote interfaith dialogue and foster a deeper understanding of Islam. Guided tours, led by knowledgeable guides, offer insights into the mosque's architecture, Islamic art, and the UAE's cultural heritage.

Practical Information for Visitors

To ensure a seamless visit to the Sheikh Zayed Grand Mosque, it is essential to have practical information at hand. Here are some key points to consider:

Opening Hours and Admission: The mosque is open to visitors daily, except on Friday mornings, which is reserved for worshippers only. Admission is free, and guided tours are available for a more enriching experience.

Dress Code and Etiquette: Modest attire is mandatory for both men and women, and women must cover their heads. Abayas and kanduras are provided at the entrance for those who need them. Photography is allowed but should be respectful and avoid capturing worshippers.

Guided Tours and Cultural Programs: The mosque offers complimentary guided tours in multiple languages, allowing visitors to explore its architectural wonders and learn about Islamic traditions. Cultural programs, such as calligraphy workshops and Quran recitation classes, are also organized regularly.

Getting There: The Sheikh Zayed Grand Mosque is located in Abu Dhabi, approximately a 90-minute drive from Dubai. Taxis, private cars, and guided tours are available for transportation.

Nearby Attractions: While visiting the mosque, consider exploring other notable attractions in Abu Dhabi, such as the Louvre Abu Dhabi, Ferrari World, and the Emirates Palace.

The Sheikh Zayed Grand Mosque stands as a testament to Dubai's grandeur and cultural heritage. Its architectural marvel, cultural significance, and religious practices make it a must-visit attraction for tourists and locals alike. Whether you are captivated by its intricate craftsmanship, seek spiritual enlightenment, or simply wish to immerse yourself in the UAE's rich cultural tapestry, the Sheikh Zayed Grand Mosque promises an unforgettable experience. As you explore Dubai, make sure to include this awe-inspiring masterpiece in your itinerary and let it leave an indelible mark on your journey through the United Arab Emirates.

•Dubai Opera

Dubai, a city known for its opulence and grandeur, offers a plethora of attractions that cater to every traveler's taste. Among its many architectural marvels, the Dubai Opera stands out as a cultural gem, captivating visitors with its world-class performances and stunning design. This comprehensive Dubai travel guide explores the essence of Dubai Opera, highlighting its historical significance, architectural brilliance, exceptional performances, and the unique experiences it offers to visitors.

I. Historical Significance and Architecture :
A. Beginnings of Dubai Opera:
Dubai Opera, located in Downtown Dubai, opened its doors to the public in August 2016. This majestic performing arts center was envisioned by Sheikh Mohammed bin Rashid Al Maktoum, the ruler of Dubai, as part of the city's ongoing commitment to promoting arts and culture.

B. Architectural Brilliance:

Dubai Opera's architecture is a captivating fusion of modern design and traditional Arabian dhow boats. The iconic dhow-inspired structure features a distinctive curved glass façade, resembling the shape of a dhow sail, which elegantly reflects the surrounding skyline and shimmering waters of Dubai Creek.

C. Interior Design:
The interior of Dubai Opera boasts world-class facilities, including a 2,000-seat auditorium that can be easily transformed into a flat-floor space for banquets and events. The venue also features cutting-edge acoustics and state-of-the-art technology to ensure optimal sound and lighting experiences for both performers and audiences.

II. Exceptional Performances :
A. Variety of Performances:
Dubai Opera has gained a reputation for hosting a diverse range of performances, including opera, ballet, classical music, contemporary concerts, theater productions, and more. International artists, renowned orchestras, and opera companies grace its stage, providing unforgettable experiences for culture enthusiasts.

B. Opera and Classical Music:

Opera aficionados can revel in the breathtaking performances of famous operas such as La Bohème, Carmen, and The Magic Flute, delivered by world-class artists and orchestras. The Dubai Opera also hosts symphony orchestras, allowing visitors to immerse themselves in the enchanting melodies of classical music.

C. Theater and Broadway Shows:
The venue showcases acclaimed theater productions and Broadway shows, bringing the magic of renowned productions like The Phantom of the Opera, Les Misérables, and The Lion King to Dubai's cultural scene.

D. Contemporary Concerts:
Dubai Opera doesn't limit itself to classical performances; it also caters to contemporary music lovers. International pop stars, rock bands, and famous musicians often grace the stage, entertaining audiences with electrifying performances.

III. Unique Experiences and Facilities :
A. Backstage Tours:
Dubai Opera offers an exclusive opportunity for visitors to go behind the scenes and discover the inner workings of this magnificent venue.

Backstage tours allow guests to explore the dressing rooms, green rooms, rehearsal spaces, and learn about the technical aspects of staging world-class performances.

B. The Rooftop Garden:
One of Dubai Opera's standout features is its rooftop garden, which offers breathtaking panoramic views of the Dubai skyline and the iconic Burj Khalifa. This serene oasis provides visitors with a tranquil space to relax and enjoy the beauty of the city.

C. Restaurants and Dining:
Dubai Opera is home to several restaurants and dining options that cater to diverse culinary preferences. Visitors can savor gourmet cuisine while enjoying spectacular views of the Dubai Fountain and Burj Khalifa, creating an unforgettable dining experience.

D. Opera Gallery:
Within the opera house, the Opera Gallery showcases a collection of stunning artworks, including paintings, sculptures, and photographs. This curated space celebrates the fusion of art and culture, providing visitors with a visual feast.

IV. Practical Information and Tips :

A. Ticket Booking:
To ensure availability, it is advisable to book tickets in advance for performances at Dubai Opera. Tickets can be purchased online through the official Dubai Opera website or through authorized ticketing partners.

B. Dress Code:
Dubai Opera maintains a smart-casual dress code, where elegant attire is encouraged for opera performances. However, for other events, the dress code may vary, and visitors are advised to check the specific requirements for each performance.

C. Accessibility:
Dubai Opera strives to be accessible to all visitors. The venue offers wheelchair-accessible seating and facilities, and staff members are readily available to assist individuals with special needs or requirements.

D. Getting There:
Dubai Opera is conveniently located in Downtown Dubai, and various transportation options are available. Visitors can use taxis, ride-sharing services, or utilize the Dubai Metro, with the Burj

Khalifa/Dubai Mall Station serving as the closest metro stop.

Dubai Opera stands as a testament to Dubai's commitment to promoting arts and culture. With its awe-inspiring architecture, exceptional performances, and unique experiences, this cultural landmark has become one of Dubai's top attractions. Whether you're an opera enthusiast, a lover of classical music, or simply seeking a memorable experience in Dubai, a visit to Dubai Opera promises to be a captivating journey into the world of performing arts. Immerse yourself in its grandeur, witness extraordinary performances, and let Dubai Opera leave an indelible mark on your travel memories.

• *Desert Safari*

Dubai, a city of towering skyscrapers, luxurious resorts, and world-class entertainment, is renowned for its diverse range of attractions. Among these, the desert safari stands out as a quintessential Dubai experience, offering a unique blend of adventure, cultural immersion, and natural beauty. This travel guide explores the enchanting world of desert safaris in Dubai, providing comprehensive insights into this top attraction.

Unveiling the Desert Safari

Dubai's desert safari is a thrilling adventure that takes visitors on a mesmerizing journey into the heart of the Arabian Desert. With its vast expanse of golden sand dunes, the desert serves as an awe-inspiring backdrop for various activities and experiences. The safari typically begins with a thrilling 4x4 dune bashing session, where expert drivers navigate through the undulating dunes, providing an adrenaline-pumping ride.

Sunset Spectacle

One of the most enchanting moments during a desert safari is witnessing the sunset over the desert horizon. The desert landscape is bathed in hues of orange and gold, creating a surreal ambiance. Travelers can capture breathtaking photographs, marvel at the vastness of the desert, or simply immerse themselves in the tranquility of the surroundings.

Traditional Arabian Hospitality

Desert safaris offer a glimpse into the rich Bedouin heritage and traditional Arabian hospitality. Upon arrival at the desert camp, visitors are greeted with dates and Arabic coffee, a customary welcome gesture. The camp, designed in a Bedouin style, provides a unique cultural experience, complete with traditional decorations, entertainment, and cuisine.

Adventure Activities

The desert safari offers an array of exhilarating activities suitable for all ages. One can embark on an adrenaline-fueled quad biking adventure, zooming across the vast sand dunes. Alternatively, sandboarding provides an opportunity to surf down the dunes, adding an element of excitement to the experience.

Camel riding is another popular activity, allowing visitors to traverse the desert in a traditional manner. Riding atop these gentle creatures provides a glimpse into the historical mode of transportation in the desert.

Cultural Experiences

To fully immerse in the Arabian culture, desert safaris provide a range of cultural experiences. Henna painting, an ancient form of body art, allows visitors to adorn their hands with intricate and temporary designs. Dressing in traditional Arabic attire, such as the flowing dishdasha for men and colorful abayas for women, adds to the authenticity of the experience.

Live performances showcase traditional dance forms, such as belly dancing and tanoura shows. The rhythmic movements and vibrant costumes captivate the audience, offering an unforgettable spectacle.

Culinary Delights

A desert safari is incomplete without savoring the delectable flavors of Arabian cuisine. The buffet-style dinner offers a diverse range of dishes, including grilled meats, aromatic rice, traditional Middle Eastern salads, and an assortment of desserts. Travelers can also indulge in freshly brewed Arabic coffee and try their hand at smoking shisha, a flavored tobacco pipe.

Stargazing and Overnight Camping

For those seeking a more immersive experience, overnight camping in the desert is an ideal option. After the thrilling activities and cultural experiences, visitors can relax around a campfire, under a blanket of stars. The clear desert skies provide an excellent opportunity for stargazing and connecting with the tranquility of nature.

A desert safari in Dubai is a must-do experience for travelers seeking adventure, cultural immersion, and natural beauty. From heart-pounding dune bashing to camel riding and traditional entertainment, the desert safari offers an unforgettable journey into the Arabian Desert. It allows visitors to appreciate the traditional Bedouin heritage while indulging in exhilarating activities and savoring mouthwatering Arabian cuisine. Whether you're an adventure enthusiast or a culture lover, a desert safari in Dubai is sure to create lasting memories of your visit to this dazzling city.

CHAPTER FOUR

Shopping in Dubai

• *Souks and Traditional Markets*

Dubai, a mesmerizing city in the United Arab Emirates, is renowned for its ultramodern architecture, luxurious shopping malls, and vibrant cultural scene. However, amidst the glitz and glamour, Dubai has managed to preserve its traditional charm through its bustling souks and traditional markets. These vibrant marketplaces offer a unique opportunity to immerse oneself in the rich cultural heritage of the region while engaging in the age-old tradition of haggling and discovering hidden gems. In this Dubai travel guide, we will take you on a captivating journey through the enchanting souks and traditional markets that have captivated visitors for centuries.

Deira Gold Souk
Our exploration begins in the heart of Dubai's historic district, Deira, where the famous Gold Souk beckons with its dazzling array of gold, diamonds,

and precious gemstones. Step into a world of opulence as you wander through narrow alleyways lined with over 300 shops, each showcasing their finest jewelry creations. From traditional Arabic designs to contemporary masterpieces, the Gold Souk is a treasure trove for jewelry enthusiasts and a delight for those seeking a cultural experience. The souk is known for its excellent craftsmanship, and visitors can even witness artisans meticulously creating intricate pieces. Whether you're looking to make a purchase or simply admire the sheer brilliance of the displays, a visit to the Deira Gold Souk is a must.

Spice Souk
Adjacent to the Gold Souk lies the aromatic Spice Souk, a sensory delight for food lovers and curious explorers. As you enter, be prepared for a sensory overload as the air is filled with the rich aroma of exotic spices, dried fruits, and traditional herbs. This bustling marketplace is a haven for gastronomes and offers an array of spices, teas, saffron, dates, and more. Engage in friendly banter with the passionate shopkeepers as they share the secrets of ancient remedies and local culinary traditions. Whether you're a seasoned chef or an amateur cook, a visit to the Spice Souk is sure to ignite your culinary senses and leave you with a

newfound appreciation for the flavors of the Middle East.

Perfume Souk

Located in the historic district of Al Ras, the Perfume Souk is a fragrant oasis where ancient perfumery traditions still thrive. Step into a world of captivating scents as you explore shops brimming with exquisite Arabian oud, incense, attars, and modern designer fragrances. The Perfume Souk is a treasure trove for fragrance connoisseurs, offering a range of unique blends that capture the essence of the Arabian Gulf. Engage in personalized consultations with knowledgeable perfumers who can help you discover your signature scent or create a bespoke fragrance tailored to your preferences. Immerse yourself in the rich olfactory heritage of the region and leave with a fragrant souvenir that will forever evoke memories of your time in Dubai.

Textile Souk

To experience the vibrant tapestry of Dubai's textile traditions, head to the Textile Souk in Bur Dubai. This hidden gem is a haven for fabric enthusiasts, with shops showcasing a kaleidoscope of colors, patterns, and textures. From luxurious silks and delicate lace to intricately embroidered fabrics and traditional Arabian garments, the Textile Souk offers a glimpse into the rich cultural heritage of the region. Bargain hunters can put their haggling skills to the test as they navigate through an assortment of shops, each offering unique textiles at competitive prices. Whether you're looking to purchase fabrics, traditional costumes, or even get a custom-made garment, the Textile Souk is a treasure trove for fashion enthusiasts and those seeking to embrace Dubai's sartorial heritage.

Souk Madinat Jumeirah

For a modern twist on traditional marketplaces, a visit to Souk Madinat Jumeirah is a must. Nestled against the backdrop of the iconic Burj Al Arab, this picturesque market seamlessly blends traditional Arabic architecture with contemporary design elements. As you stroll through its meandering alleyways, you'll find a curated selection of boutiques, art galleries, and souvenir shops offering an eclectic mix of traditional crafts, handmade jewelry, carpets, and artworks. After indulging in some retail therapy, unwind at one of the souk's many restaurants or cafes, offering a variety of cuisines from around the world. The serene waterways and stunning views of the Arabian Gulf make Souk Madinat Jumeirah an ideal place to relax, shop, and soak in the ambiance of modern Dubai.

Dubai's souks and traditional markets provide a captivating glimpse into the city's rich cultural heritage. From the glimmering gold of the Deira Gold Souk to the tantalizing aromas of the Spice Souk and the fragrant allure of the Perfume Souk, these vibrant marketplaces offer an enchanting journey through Dubai's past and present. The Textile Souk showcases the region's artistic prowess through its diverse range of fabrics, while Souk Madinat Jumeirah offers a contemporary twist on traditional markets. Exploring these markets not only allows visitors to find unique souvenirs and treasures but also provides an opportunity to interact with local shopkeepers, immerse themselves in the traditions of the region, and create lasting memories of their Dubai experience. So, whether you're a shopaholic, a culture enthusiast, or a curious traveler, don't miss the chance to discover the magic of Dubai's souks and traditional markets.

• *Luxury Shopping Malls*

Dubai, known for its opulence and grandeur, is a haven for luxury shopping enthusiasts from around the world. With its iconic skyline, breathtaking architecture, and extravagant lifestyle, Dubai boasts some of the most prestigious and extravagant shopping malls on the planet. In this comprehensive travel guide, we will explore the captivating world of luxury shopping malls in Dubai, where visitors can indulge in high-end retail therapy and immerse themselves in a world of luxury and glamour.

The Dubai Mall:

We begin our journey with the crown jewel of Dubai's shopping scene, The Dubai Mall. As the largest mall in the world by total area, this prestigious shopping destination offers an unparalleled luxury shopping experience. With over 1,300 retail outlets, including the world's most renowned luxury brands, visitors can explore an extensive range of high-end fashion, jewelry, accessories, and more. The mall also houses the iconic Fashion Avenue, a dedicated precinct for luxury shopping, where exclusive flagship stores of top fashion brands are located.

Mall of the Emirates:
Next on our list is the Mall of the Emirates, a prominent shopping destination renowned for its luxurious offerings. This mall is home to over 700 high-end retailers, including international luxury brands, designer boutiques, and department stores. What sets Mall of the Emirates apart is its renowned Fashion Dome, an exquisite section of the mall dedicated to luxury fashion, where visitors can discover the latest collections from prestigious designers.

The Avenue at Etihad Towers:
For those seeking a sophisticated and exclusive shopping experience, The Avenue at Etihad Towers is a must-visit destination. Situated in Abu Dhabi, just a short drive from Dubai, this luxurious shopping complex offers a curated selection of high-end brands, luxury goods, and upscale dining options. The elegant and refined ambiance, combined with breathtaking views of the Arabian Gulf, creates an unforgettable shopping experience.

City Walk:
Moving away from traditional mall settings, City Walk presents a unique outdoor shopping and lifestyle experience. Located in the heart of Dubai, this upscale retail destination combines luxury

shopping with entertainment and dining. City Walk features a carefully designed urban space with beautifully landscaped streets, trendy boutiques, and flagship stores of renowned fashion labels. Visitors can enjoy a leisurely stroll while exploring the latest fashion trends, avant-garde art galleries, and indulging in exquisite dining options.

Wafi Mall:
A true architectural gem, Wafi Mall is an Egyptian-themed shopping destination that exudes luxury and grandeur. Inspired by ancient Egyptian design, the mall houses an exquisite collection of high-end boutiques and luxury brands, offering visitors a truly unique shopping experience. Wafi Mall is also home to the renowned Khan Murjan Souk, a recreation of a traditional Middle Eastern market, where visitors can explore an array of handicrafts, jewelry, and authentic Arabian treasures.

The Galleria:
Situated on the iconic Al Maryah Island in Abu Dhabi, The Galleria offers an unrivaled luxury shopping experience in a stunning waterfront setting. Boasting a selection of high-end fashion boutiques, designer stores, and world-class dining establishments, this upscale mall caters to the most

discerning shoppers. With its breathtaking architecture, luxurious ambiance, and a plethora of prestigious brands, The Galleria is a haven for luxury connoisseurs.

Dubai's luxury shopping malls provide an unmatched experience for discerning shoppers seeking the epitome of opulence. With their grand architecture, vast retail offerings, and world-class amenities, these malls redefine the concept of luxury shopping. From The Dubai Mall's extravagance to the exclusive boutiques at The Avenue, and the unique outdoor experience at City Walk, Dubai offers a remarkable range of luxury shopping destinations. Whether you're a fashion enthusiast, a jewelry connoisseur, or simply seeking an unforgettable retail experience, Dubai's luxury shopping malls are sure to captivate and indulge your senses in the lap of ultimate luxury.

- *Dubai Duty-Free*

Dubai, the vibrant and cosmopolitan city nestled in the United Arab Emirates (UAE), is renowned for its architectural wonders, luxurious lifestyle, and unparalleled shopping experiences. Among the many remarkable shopping destinations in Dubai, one name stands out - Dubai Duty-Free. Located in Dubai International Airport, Dubai Duty-Free has earned a well-deserved reputation as a shopper's paradise, offering a wide range of products, excellent customer service, and a tax-free shopping experience. This comprehensive travel guide explores the myriad attractions and features of Dubai Duty-Free, making it an essential stop for any visitor to this remarkable city.

Overview of Dubai Duty-Free:
Spanning an impressive area of over 38,000 square meters, Dubai Duty-Free has become one of the world's largest airport retailers. It caters to the needs and desires of both international travelers and local residents alike. Since its inception in 1983, Dubai Duty-Free has garnered numerous accolades for its outstanding retail offerings and premium services.

Shopping Extravaganza:
Dubai Duty-Free boasts an extensive array of shopping options across various categories,

ensuring there is something for every taste and preference. From high-end luxury brands to locally crafted souvenirs, shoppers can indulge in a diverse range of products such as perfumes, cosmetics, electronics, fashion, jewelry, watches, confectionery, liquor, and tobacco. The duty-free prices make it an irresistible shopping destination for tourists seeking premium products at competitive rates.

Luxury at its Finest:
Dubai Duty-Free is synonymous with luxury, and this is evident in its prestigious boutiques and upscale brands. The Perfume and Cosmetics section is a haven for beauty enthusiasts, featuring renowned brands like Chanel, Dior, Tom Ford, and Estée Lauder. The Fashion section showcases international designers, including Burberry, Gucci, Louis Vuitton, and Prada. For those seeking fine jewelry and watches, iconic brands like Rolex, Cartier, and Tiffany & Co. offer an unmatched shopping experience.

Electronics and Gadgets Galore:
Tech-savvy travelers will be delighted by the extensive range of electronic gadgets available at Dubai Duty-Free. From smartphones, tablets, and laptops to the latest gaming consoles and audio

equipment, the Electronics section caters to all tech-related needs. Brands like Apple, Samsung, Sony, and Bose are just a few of the prominent names offering their products in this section.

Culinary Delights:
Dubai Duty-Free ensures that shoppers' taste buds are satisfied with its diverse culinary offerings. The Food and Confectionery section presents an assortment of gourmet treats, chocolates, and candies from renowned brands such as Godiva, Lindt, and Toblerone. Travelers can also savor a variety of international cuisines in the Food Court, with options ranging from fast food to fine dining experiences.

Exclusive Offers and Promotions:
Dubai Duty-Free continuously provides exclusive offers and promotions, further enhancing the shopping experience for visitors. Special events, seasonal sales, and raffles offering luxurious prizes create a sense of excitement and make shopping at Dubai Duty-Free even more enticing.

Convenience and Customer Service:
Apart from its extensive product range, Dubai Duty-Free prioritizes convenience and customer satisfaction. The airport's strategic layout ensures

easy accessibility, with dedicated areas for arrivals and departures. Friendly and knowledgeable staff are readily available to assist shoppers with their queries and provide guidance throughout the shopping journey. Additionally, Dubai Duty-Free offers services like personal shoppers, home delivery, and tax refunds, ensuring a seamless and enjoyable experience.

Dubai Duty-Free Millennium Millionaire:
One of the most iconic features of Dubai Duty-Free is the Millennium Millionaire promotion. Travelers have the chance to win one million US dollars in the Millennium Millionaire draw by purchasing tickets for the raffle. This promotion has not only garnered global recognition but has also contributed to numerous success stories of lucky winners.

Supporting Charitable Causes:
Dubai Duty-Free is committed to giving back to the community through its extensive Corporate Social Responsibility initiatives. It supports various charitable causes, including children's hospitals, medical centers, and educational institutions, making a positive impact on society.

Beyond Shopping: Dubai International Airport:

Dubai Duty-Free's location within Dubai International Airport allows visitors to explore the airport's myriad attractions. From world-class lounges and luxurious spas to immersive art installations and captivating exhibitions, Dubai International Airport offers an all-encompassing experience beyond shopping.

Dubai Duty-Free stands as a testament to Dubai's dedication to providing exceptional shopping experiences. With its vast selection of luxury brands, diverse product offerings, exclusive promotions, and exceptional customer service, Dubai Duty-Free continues to captivate visitors from around the globe. Whether you are a tourist passing through Dubai International Airport or a resident seeking the finest products, Dubai Duty-Free promises an unforgettable shopping journey. Indulge in a world of luxury and convenience, and discover why Dubai Duty-Free truly is a shopper's paradise in the heart of Dubai.

•*Gold Souk*

Dubai, the dazzling metropolis of the United Arab Emirates, is renowned for its opulence, architectural marvels, and vibrant cultural heritage. Among its many treasures, the Gold Souk stands out as an iconic destination that epitomizes Dubai's status as the "City of Gold." Nestled in the heart of Deira, the historic district, the Gold Souk is a mesmerizing marketplace that lures visitors from around the world with its glittering displays of gold, intricate craftsmanship, and timeless beauty. This comprehensive Dubai travel guide unveils the captivating allure of the Gold Souk, providing insights into its rich history, vibrant atmosphere, shopping experiences, and essential tips for a memorable visit.

I. A Glimpse into the History

Dubai's association with gold dates back centuries, rooted in its heritage as a vibrant trading hub. The Gold Souk traces its origins to the early 1900s when a small number of local traders set up shops along the creek. Over time, the Gold Souk grew in prominence, becoming a hub for gold trade and attracting merchants from across the region. Today, it stands as one of the largest gold markets globally, showcasing an incredible range of jewelry, gemstones, and precious metals.

II. A Feast for the Senses

Stepping into the Gold Souk is an assault on the senses, where the sparkle of gold catches the eye, and the vibrant sounds of haggling fill the air. The labyrinthine alleyways are lined with a dazzling array of shops, each brimming with exquisite designs crafted by skilled artisans. From traditional Emirati designs to contemporary creations, the Gold Souk offers an unparalleled selection of gold jewelry, including necklaces, bracelets, earrings, rings, and intricately embellished watches.

III. Expertise and Authenticity
One of the key aspects that sets the Gold Souk apart is its commitment to quality and authenticity. Gold sold in the souk is regulated by the Dubai government, ensuring that each piece meets stringent purity standards. Visitors can be assured of the authenticity of their purchases, as every item is stamped with the karatage, indicating its gold content. Additionally, many shops in the Gold Souk employ expert jewelers who can customize designs or guide customers in selecting the perfect piece.

IV. Beyond Gold: Gems and Precious Stones
While gold reigns supreme in the Gold Souk, it also boasts a remarkable collection of precious gemstones. Visitors can feast their eyes on an array of vibrant rubies, dazzling diamonds, mesmerizing

sapphires, and a myriad of other precious stones. Whether one seeks a statement necklace adorned with emeralds or a pair of delicate pearl earrings, the Gold Souk offers an extensive selection to suit every taste and budget.

V. Unveiling the Shopping Experience
Exploring the Gold Souk is not just about making purchases; it's a cultural experience in itself. Haggling is an accepted practice, and visitors can engage in friendly negotiations to secure the best prices. It's important to approach haggling with a smile and a respectful attitude, as it is part of the local culture. Bargaining is often done with good humor and can lead to memorable interactions with the friendly shopkeepers.

VI. Practical Tips for Visitors
To make the most of a visit to the Gold Souk, it's essential to keep a few practical tips in mind. First and foremost, it's advisable to visit during weekdays when the market is less crowded. The Gold Souk is easily accessible via public transportation, and parking facilities are available nearby. Visitors should also be mindful of their belongings and keep an eye on their personal belongings, as the market can get crowded at peak hours.

Dubai's Gold Souk is a mesmerizing destination that enthralls visitors with its grandeur, artistic mastery, and cultural significance. It is not just a marketplace; it's a treasure trove where dreams are brought to life in the form of exquisite jewelry and precious metals. The experience of wandering through its enchanting lanes, haggling with shopkeepers, and discovering unique designs is an adventure in itself. Whether one is a seasoned jewelry connoisseur or a curious traveler, the Gold Souk is an absolute must-visit. It encapsulates the essence of Dubai's rich heritage while showcasing the city's penchant for luxury and extravagance. Exploring the Gold Souk in Dubai is an unforgettable experience, and every visitor is sure to leave with a piece of this shimmering gem in their heart.

•*Spice Souk*

Dubai, a city known for its opulent skyscrapers, luxurious shopping malls, and extravagant lifestyle, also offers a taste of the traditional and exotic. Tucked away in the heart of Old Dubai, amidst the bustling streets and historic neighborhoods, lies a treasure trove of fragrances and flavors—the Spice

Souk. This vibrant market is a haven for spice enthusiasts, culinary explorers, and curious travelers seeking an authentic cultural experience. In this comprehensive Dubai travel guide, we delve into the enchanting world of the Spice Souk, revealing its history, highlights, and tips for navigating through this aromatic maze.

Unveiling the Heritage :

Dubai's Spice Souk has a rich history dating back to the early days of the city's trading culture. In the past, the market served as a hub for merchants from all over the world, offering an extensive range of spices, herbs, and traditional medicinal products. Today, the souk continues to thrive, showcasing its enduring heritage and welcoming visitors with its vibrant atmosphere.

Getting There :

Located in Deira, one of Dubai's oldest neighborhoods, the Spice Souk is easily accessible by various modes of transportation. Travelers can opt for a traditional abra (water taxi) ride across the Dubai Creek, providing a picturesque journey to the souk. Alternatively, taxis and public buses offer convenient options for reaching the market.

Sensory Delights :

Upon entering the Spice Souk, visitors are immediately immersed in a sensory extravaganza. The vibrant colors, fragrant aromas, and lively sounds create a captivating ambiance. Spice stalls line the narrow alleyways, showcasing an incredible assortment of spices from across the globe. Saffron, cinnamon, cardamom, cloves, turmeric, and countless other spices are elegantly displayed, enticing visitors to explore and indulge in their aromatic wonders.

Hidden Gems and Unique Offerings :

While the Spice Souk predominantly focuses on spices, it also offers a diverse array of other products. Visitors can find traditional perfumes (attars), incense, dried fruits, nuts, and local delicacies. Exploring the souk's hidden corners, one may stumble upon stalls selling exotic teas, herbal remedies, and medicinal products. It's a paradise for those seeking unusual and unique souvenirs.

Haggling and Bargaining :

The art of haggling is deeply embedded in the Middle Eastern culture, and the Spice Souk is no exception. Bargaining is not only expected but also adds an element of excitement to the shopping experience. Visitors should engage in friendly negotiation, keeping in mind that the final price should be fair to both parties.

Culinary Inspiration :
The Spice Souk is a paradise for culinary enthusiasts. The vast selection of spices provides an opportunity to discover new flavors and enhance culinary skills. Visitors can engage in conversations with the local vendors, who are often passionate about their products and eager to share their knowledge and culinary secrets. They can offer recommendations, advice, and even recipes, enabling travelers to bring the flavors of Dubai back home.

Exploring Beyond the Souk :
While the Spice Souk is a captivating destination on its own, visitors can further explore the surrounding area. The nearby Gold Souk, with its dazzling displays of gold and precious jewelry, offers a glimpse into Dubai's thriving trade industry. Travelers can also venture into the surrounding alleyways, discovering traditional Emirati architecture, historic mosques, and lively markets, providing a deeper understanding of Dubai's cultural heritage.

Practical Tips and Etiquette :

To make the most of the Spice Souk experience, it's helpful to keep a few practical tips in mind. Dress modestly to respect local customs, especially in this conservative neighborhood. Bring cash, as many vendors may not accept card payments. Take your time to explore and compare prices before making a purchase, as the variety of stalls ensures competitive pricing.

The Spice Souk in Dubai is a captivating destination that offers a unique sensory experience and a window into the city's rich heritage. From the vibrant colors and fragrant aromas to the warm hospitality of the vendors, every moment spent in this enchanting market is a celebration of culture and tradition. Whether you are a seasoned chef seeking exotic ingredients or an intrepid traveler yearning for an authentic encounter, the Spice Souk is a must-visit destination that will leave an indelible mark on your Dubai journey. So, embrace the intoxicating aromas, engage in friendly haggling, and let the Spice Souk ignite your senses with its flavorsome treasures.

• ***Dubai Shopping Festival***

Dubai, the crown jewel of the United Arab Emirates, has become synonymous with luxury, opulence, and world-class shopping experiences. Among its many spectacular attractions, the Dubai Shopping Festival (DSF) stands out as a retail extravaganza that draws millions of visitors from around the globe. In this comprehensive Dubai travel guide, we will explore the vibrant and exciting world of the Dubai Shopping Festival, offering insights into its history, attractions, and tips for making the most of this shopaholic's dream.

The Origins and Evolution of the Dubai Shopping Festival

The Dubai Shopping Festival was first launched in 1996 as a government initiative to boost tourism and trade in the city. Over the years, it has evolved into one of the world's most significant shopping events, attracting shopaholics, bargain hunters, and fashion enthusiasts alike. The festival usually takes place during the first quarter of the year, transforming the city into a vibrant shopping paradise for a month-long extravaganza.

DSF Highlights and Attractions

The Dubai Shopping Festival offers a multitude of attractions that cater to every visitor's preferences. From high-end luxury brands to traditional marketplaces, there is something for everyone. The festival is renowned for its spectacular fireworks, fashion shows, live concerts, street performances, and cultural events that add to the celebratory atmosphere. Global Village, an expansive multicultural shopping and entertainment destination, is a must-visit during DSF, offering a glimpse into different cultures through food, crafts, and performances.

Shopping Venues and Experiences
Dubai boasts a plethora of shopping venues that come alive during the festival. The city is home to iconic malls like the Dubai Mall, Mall of the Emirates, and Ibn Battuta Mall, which offer a vast array of international brands, designer boutiques, and flagship stores. Bargain hunters can explore traditional souks such as the Gold Souk, Spice Souk, and Textile Souk, where haggling for gold, spices, fabrics, and souvenirs is an art form.

Unmissable Deals and Promotions
During the Dubai Shopping Festival, visitors can indulge in unbeatable deals, discounts, and promotions across various retail categories. From

fashion and electronics to cosmetics and home furnishings, shoppers can enjoy significant savings and exclusive offers. Many brands and retailers launch new collections and products during the festival, providing an excellent opportunity for fashion-forward individuals to stay ahead of the trends.

Food and Entertainment

The Dubai Shopping Festival is not just about shopping; it's a holistic experience that delights all the senses. Food enthusiasts can savor a diverse range of international cuisines at the festival's food stalls, pop-up restaurants, and food trucks. The festival also hosts live performances by renowned artists, including musicians, dancers, and cultural troupes, ensuring visitors are entertained throughout their shopping spree.

Tips for Navigating the Dubai Shopping Festival

To make the most of the Dubai Shopping Festival, it is essential to plan ahead and strategize. Researching the best deals, creating a budget, and identifying preferred shopping venues can help streamline the experience. Visitors should also consider timing their visit to coincide with major events and attractions during the festival.

Additionally, understanding the local customs and traditions will enhance the overall experience and foster a deeper connection with the city and its people.

The Dubai Shopping Festival is an unparalleled shopping extravaganza that showcases Dubai's penchant for luxury, innovation, and grandeur. With its exceptional retail offerings, exciting events, and festive ambiance, the festival has firmly established Dubai as a premier global shopping destination. Whether you are a fashion enthusiast, a tech aficionado, or simply a lover of vibrant cultures, the Dubai Shopping Festival promises an unforgettable experience. So, pack your bags, ready your wallets, and embark on a retail adventure like no other in the mesmerizing city of Dubai.

CHAPTER FIVE

Dining and Cuisine

• *Local Emirati Cuisine*

Dubai, the dazzling city of the United Arab Emirates, is renowned for its remarkable blend of diverse cultures, extravagant architecture, and luxurious lifestyle. Amidst the towering skyscrapers and bustling city streets, Dubai hides a culinary treasure trove that is often overlooked by visitors. Local Emirati cuisine, rooted in the traditional Bedouin culture and influenced by various international flavors, offers a remarkable gastronomic experience that is worth exploring. In this Dubai travel guide, we delve into the rich tapestry of Emirati cuisine, highlighting its key dishes, unique ingredients, and best places to savor the authentic flavors of Dubai.

Historical and Cultural Influences:

Emirati cuisine is deeply rooted in the region's history, traditions, and Bedouin way of life. It reflects the heritage of the Bedouin people who relied on their nomadic lifestyle, engaging in fishing, pearl diving, and herding livestock. Over time, Dubai's cuisine has been influenced by traders from Persia, India, and other parts of the Arabian Peninsula. This confluence of cultures has shaped the diverse flavors found in Emirati dishes.

Key Ingredients and Spices:
Emirati cuisine showcases a harmonious blend of fresh seafood, succulent meats, aromatic spices, and fragrant herbs. Some key ingredients that form the basis of many dishes include dates, camel meat, fish, rice, wheat, saffron, cardamom, turmeric, and rosewater. The use of these ingredients adds depth and complexity to the flavors, creating a unique culinary experience.

Traditional Emirati Dishes:
a) Machboos: Considered the national dish of the United Arab Emirates, Machboos is a flavorful rice dish typically prepared with meat, such as lamb, chicken, or fish. It is seasoned with a blend of spices, including turmeric, cinnamon, and dried lime, giving it a distinctive aroma.

b) Harees: Harees is a traditional Emirati dish made from wheat and meat, usually chicken or lamb. The ingredients are slow-cooked to create a porridge-like consistency, resulting in a comforting and hearty dish. It is commonly enjoyed during Ramadan and other festive occasions.

c) Luqaimat: A popular Emirati dessert, Luqaimat consists of small, deep-fried dumplings drizzled with date syrup and sprinkled with sesame seeds. These sweet and sticky treats are perfect for satisfying your sweet tooth.

d) Majboos Samak: As a coastal city, Dubai offers an array of delicious seafood dishes. Majboos Samak is a spicy fish dish cooked with rice, tomatoes, and a blend of aromatic spices. The fish is typically marinated and then pan-fried to perfection.

Traditional Emirati Beverages:
a) Gahwa: Gahwa, or Arabic coffee, is an integral part of Emirati hospitality and is often served to guests as a welcome gesture. This strong and aromatic coffee is made from lightly roasted Arabica beans and is flavored with cardamom. It is traditionally served in small cups accompanied by dates.

b) Laban: Laban, a refreshing yogurt-based drink, is popular in Emirati cuisine. It is often served chilled and can be enjoyed plain or flavored with mint, rosewater, or saffron. Laban helps to balance the spices in Emirati dishes and provides a cooling effect.

Where to Experience Local Emirati Cuisine:
a) Al Fanar Restaurant and Cafe: Located in Dubai Festival City, Al Fanar offers a truly authentic Emirati dining experience. The restaurant's decor transports you to a traditional Emirati home, while the menu features a wide range of classic Emirati dishes, ensuring a delightful gastronomic journey..

b) Local Markets and Food Stalls: Exploring local markets, such as the Spice Souk and the Fish Market, provides an opportunity to sample Emirati street food and snacks. Food stalls offer dishes like shawarma, falafel, and samosas, providing a taste of both Emirati and Middle Eastern flavors.

c) Sheikh Mohammed Centre for Cultural Understanding: This cultural center organizes heritage tours and cultural meals where visitors can learn about Emirati traditions, customs, and cuisine. It offers an immersive experience that deepens your understanding of Emirati culture.

Dubai's culinary scene extends far beyond international cuisines and Michelin-starred restaurants. Exploring the local Emirati cuisine in Dubai offers a glimpse into the rich cultural heritage of the city. From savory rice dishes to aromatic spices and sweet delicacies, Emirati cuisine is a fusion of flavors that reflects Dubai's historical roots. So, as you embark on your journey through this cosmopolitan city, don't miss the opportunity to savor the authentic tastes of Emirati cuisine and immerse yourself in the local culinary traditions.

•*International Cuisine*

Dubai, the dazzling metropolis in the United Arab Emirates, is known for its opulent skyscrapers, luxurious resorts, and vibrant culture. Beyond its architectural marvels and desert landscapes, Dubai is also a hub of diverse culinary experiences. As a melting pot of cultures and nationalities, the city offers an extraordinary array of international cuisines that cater to every palate. In this Dubai travel guide, we embark on a gastronomic adventure to explore the rich tapestry of international flavors that await you in this vibrant city.

Arabic Delights:
Dubai's culinary scene is deeply rooted in its Arabic heritage, offering an abundance of traditional Middle Eastern delights. Indulge in the aromatic flavors of dishes like hummus, falafel, tabbouleh, and fattoush, which are found in numerous restaurants and street food stalls across the city. Be sure to savor the succulent grilled meats, such as shawarma and kebabs, prepared with a delightful blend of spices. Additionally, a visit to a traditional Emirati restaurant will introduce you to local specialties like Machboos (spiced rice with meat), Harees (a porridge-like dish), and Luqaimat (sweet dumplings).

Levantine Cuisine:
Dubai serves as a gateway to the Levant region, encompassing the culinary traditions of Lebanon, Syria, Jordan, and Palestine. Discover the vibrant flavors of Levantine cuisine by relishing the savory delights of mezze platters, featuring dishes like baba ganoush, moutabel, and labneh. Delight in the mouthwatering grills, such as shish taouk (marinated chicken skewers) and kofta (seasoned ground meat). For a taste of authentic Levantine

street food, visit the bustling Al Mallah restaurant or explore the vibrant food stalls in the Old Dubai area.

Asian Fusion:
Dubai's multicultural makeup is further celebrated through its diverse Asian culinary offerings. From Chinese and Japanese to Thai and Indian, the city boasts an impressive range of Asian fusion restaurants. Savor the delicate flavors of sushi and sashimi in upscale Japanese establishments, or dive into the fiery spices of Thai curries and stir-fries. Dubai's Little India district, also known as Meena Bazaar, is a haven for Indian cuisine lovers, where you can enjoy traditional biryanis, butter chicken, and an array of vegetarian delights.

Continental Delicacies:
Dubai's cosmopolitan atmosphere is mirrored in its selection of Continental cuisines. From French and Italian to Spanish and British, the city is home to world-class restaurants that cater to every taste. Indulge in fine dining experiences at Michelin-starred venues, sample artisanal cheeses and freshly baked bread in charming European-style cafes, or treat yourself to decadent desserts from renowned pastry shops. Dubai's Marina and Downtown areas are particularly

famous for their impressive selection of upscale restaurants offering an international culinary journey.

African and South American Influences:
Dubai's culinary scene extends its reach to the vibrant flavors of Africa and South America. Experience the robust spices of Moroccan tagines, the soulful stews of Ethiopia, and the aromatic specialties of South Africa. Sample Brazilian churrasco, Argentinean steaks, and Peruvian ceviche in Dubai's Latin American restaurants, which artfully blend traditional recipes with contemporary techniques.

The Sweet Side of Dubai:
No culinary exploration in Dubai would be complete without a venture into the world of sweets and desserts. From traditional Emirati sweets like baklava and kunafa to French pastries, Turkish delights, and Indian sweets, Dubai presents a tantalizing array of sweet indulgences. Don't miss a visit to the city's popular dessert destinations, such as the Arabian Tea House, where you can enjoy a cup of aromatic tea accompanied by a delectable selection of local treats.

Dubai's international cuisine scene is a testament to the city's diverse and cosmopolitan nature. Whether you're a fan of Middle Eastern flavors, Asian delights, or continental delicacies, Dubai offers an unparalleled culinary journey that will leave your taste buds craving for more. Embrace the opportunity to explore the rich tapestry of international flavors and embark on a gastronomic adventure in this captivating city, where the world's cuisines come together in a vibrant melting pot.

• *Street Food*

Dubai, a city known for its opulence, grandeur, and futuristic skyline, is also a treasure trove for food enthusiasts. While Dubai is celebrated for its world-class restaurants and fine dining experiences, one cannot overlook the vibrant and diverse street food scene that thrives within its bustling streets. This comprehensive Dubai travel guide aims to delve into the culinary wonders that can be found on the city's streets, offering a tantalizing array of flavors and aromas that reflect the multiculturalism and cosmopolitan nature of Dubai.

Cultural Fusion: A Melting Pot of Flavors

Dubai's street food culture is a delightful reflection of its diverse population. As an international hub, the city has attracted people from all corners of the globe, resulting in a fusion of culinary traditions. Visitors can embark on a culinary journey around the world by sampling dishes from India, Pakistan, Lebanon, Iran, Thailand, China, and beyond. The streets of Dubai serve as a melting pot, where the fragrant spices, fresh ingredients, and authentic recipes create an explosion of flavors.

The Iconic Shawarma: A Dubai Staple
No exploration of Dubai's street food scene would be complete without mentioning the iconic shawarma. A popular Middle Eastern delight, the shawarma consists of succulent slices of marinated meat (usually chicken or lamb) grilled on a vertical spit and then wrapped in a warm pita bread. The fragrant aroma of the spices wafts through the streets, enticing locals and tourists alike. Whether enjoyed with a side of creamy garlic sauce or pickled vegetables, the shawarma is a must-try street food experience in Dubai.

Delectable Emirati Delights: Local Flavors
Dubai's street food culture also embraces traditional Emirati cuisine, offering a glimpse into the rich culinary heritage of the region. Visitors can

savor dishes like Machbous (spiced rice with meat or seafood), Luqaimat (sweet dumplings drizzled with date syrup), and Mutton Harees (a slow-cooked dish of wheat and tender mutton). These authentic Emirati flavors provide an opportunity to connect with the local culture and indulge in age-old traditions.

The Culinary Souks: A Gastronomic Adventure

To truly immerse yourself in Dubai's street food culture, a visit to the bustling culinary souks is a must. The city is home to vibrant marketplaces, such as the Spice Souk and the Deira Fish Market, where locals and visitors can interact with vendors, explore a plethora of exotic spices, and witness the lively trade of fresh produce and seafood. The experience of haggling for spices and purchasing fresh ingredients adds an element of adventure to the street food journey.

Food Trucks and Night Markets: A Modern Twist

In recent years, Dubai has embraced the global trend of food trucks and night markets, providing a contemporary twist to its street food scene. Visitors can enjoy an array of gourmet offerings, from artisanal burgers and loaded fries to fusion cuisine and decadent desserts, all served from the colorful food trucks that dot the city's streets. Night markets, such as the Ripe Market and the Dubai Flea Market, offer a festive atmosphere where one can indulge in delicious street food while shopping for unique crafts and local produce.

Dubai's street food culture is an integral part of the city's vibrant tapestry. From the tantalizing aromas of shawarmas and kebabs to the traditional flavors of Emirati cuisine, exploring the street food scene in Dubai is an adventure that engages all the senses. The city's multiculturalism and cosmopolitan nature are evident in the diverse range of culinary offerings available on its streets. Whether you are strolling through the bustling souks or savoring gourmet delights from a food truck, the street food experience in Dubai promises to be an unforgettable gastronomic journey.

As you explore the diverse flavors and aromas, remember to embrace the local customs, savor the authenticity of each dish, and engage with the friendly street food vendors who take immense pride in their craft. Dubai's street food scene is a testament to the city's ability to blend tradition and innovation, offering a culinary adventure that truly reflects the spirit of this magnificent destination. So, grab your appetite, embark on a culinary exploration, and let the vibrant street food culture of Dubai captivate your taste buds.

• *Fine Dining*

Dubai, a city synonymous with opulence and grandeur, has emerged as a global hub for fine dining. With its diverse culinary landscape and a penchant for pushing boundaries, the city offers an unparalleled gastronomic experience. From award-winning restaurants helmed by renowned chefs to luxurious venues with breathtaking views, Dubai's dining scene caters to the most discerning palates. This comprehensive Dubai travel guide delves into the world of fine dining in Dubai, showcasing the city's top-notch culinary offerings, vibrant flavors, and lavish dining experiences.

A Global Melting Pot of Cuisines

Dubai's multicultural population and its status as an international travel destination have paved the way for an eclectic culinary scene. Visitors can indulge in a myriad of cuisines, including Arabic, Indian, Persian, Mediterranean, Asian, and

European. From traditional Emirati delicacies to innovative fusion creations, Dubai's dining establishments cater to all tastes.

Michelin-Starred Excellence
Dubai boasts a growing list of Michelin-starred restaurants, attracting discerning food enthusiasts from around the world. Establishments such as Zuma, La Petite Maison, and Nobu have gained global acclaim for their exceptional culinary offerings, impeccable service, and exquisite presentation. These dining venues showcase the city's commitment to culinary excellence and are a testament to Dubai's rise as a global gastronomic destination.

Iconic Dining Destinations
Dubai's skyline is adorned with iconic landmarks, and many of these architectural marvels are home to world-class dining establishments. The Burj Khalifa, the tallest building in the world, features At.mosphere, a fine dining restaurant offering unparalleled views of the city while savoring gourmet delights. Additionally, the Burj Al Arab, an epitome of luxury, hosts Al Mahara, a seafood restaurant known for its underwater dining experience, where guests can enjoy a meal surrounded by mesmerizing marine life.

Exquisite Seafood Delights
Given its proximity to the Arabian Gulf, Dubai is a haven for seafood lovers. The city's numerous seafood restaurants serve up a plethora of fresh catches, ranging from local delicacies like hammour and prawns to international favorites like oysters and lobster. Pierchic, nestled at the end of a pier in Madinat Jumeirah, offers a romantic setting and a menu featuring the finest seafood delicacies, making it a must-visit for seafood aficionados.

Authentic Emirati Cuisine
To truly experience the local culture, visitors should savor the authentic flavors of Emirati cuisine. Dubai's heritage-themed restaurants, such as Al Fanar and Seven Sands, provide a glimpse into the traditional Emirati way of life while serving delectable dishes like Machbous (spiced rice with meat or fish) and Harees (slow-cooked wheat and meat). These establishments offer a blend of traditional recipes and warm hospitality, allowing guests to immerse themselves in the Emirati culinary heritage.

Unique Dining Experiences
Dubai is known for its innovative and unique dining concepts that go beyond just great food. The city

offers various immersive experiences, such as dining in the desert under the stars, enjoying a meal aboard a luxury yacht, or indulging in a private dinner atop the dunes. Restaurants like Pai Thai, nestled in the Madinat Jumeirah resort, offer traditional Thai cuisine served in private abra boats, creating a one-of-a-kind dining experience.

Dubai's fine dining scene presents a tantalizing array of culinary experiences that cater to every taste and preference. From Michelin-starred restaurants to iconic venues with breathtaking views, the city offers a sensory journey that tantalizes both the palate and the senses. Whether indulging in exquisite seafood, exploring diverse international cuisines, or savoring traditional Emirati dishes, visitors to Dubai are sure to embark on a gastronomic adventure like no other. With its commitment to culinary excellence and unwavering passion for innovation, Dubai continues to elevate the fine dining experience, solidifying its position as a world-class destination for epicurean delights.

•Traditional Arabic

Dubai, the bustling metropolis and cultural hub of the United Arab Emirates, is known for its glamorous skyscrapers, luxurious shopping malls, and modern architecture. However, beneath the glitz and glamour lies a rich tapestry of traditional Arabic culture that has been preserved and celebrated in this cosmopolitan city. In this comprehensive travel guide, we delve into the traditional Arabic aspects of Dubai, offering insights into the city's heritage, customs, cuisine, and experiences that will immerse you in the authentic Emirati culture.

Emirati Heritage and History:

Dubai's cultural heritage can be traced back centuries when it was a small trading port. Start your journey by visiting the Dubai Museum, located in the Al Fahidi Fort, the city's oldest building. Here, you can explore exhibits that showcase the history and traditional lifestyle of the Emirati people. Discover the ancient pearl diving industry, traditional Emirati clothing, and learn about the Bedouin way of life.

Traditional Arabic Architecture:

While Dubai is renowned for its modern architecture, there are still pockets of the city where you can admire traditional Arabic architectural gems. Al Bastakiya, the oldest residential area in Dubai, is a labyrinth of narrow lanes, wind towers, and traditional courtyard houses. Take a leisurely stroll through its alleys, visit art galleries, and enjoy the tranquility of this historic neighborhood.

Souks and Traditional Markets:
No visit to Dubai is complete without exploring the vibrant souks and traditional markets. Start with the Gold Souk, a dazzling display of gold and jewelry, where you can witness the craftsmanship and barter for exquisite pieces. Move on to the Spice Souk, filled with aromatic herbs, spices, and dried fruits. Absorb the sights, sounds, and scents of these bustling markets, and interact with local traders to learn about their age-old traditions.

Arabic Cuisine:
Indulge your taste buds in the flavors of traditional Arabic cuisine. Visit Al-Fahidi Street, where you'll find a plethora of local eateries serving authentic Emirati dishes. Try dishes like Machbous (spiced rice with meat), Harees (wheat and meat porridge), and Luqaimat (sweet dumplings). Embrace the dining etiquette of eating with your right hand and

savor the rich spices and flavors that make Arabic cuisine so unique.

Arabic Hospitality and Traditions:
Hospitality is a cornerstone of Arabic culture, and Dubai is no exception. Experience Emirati warmth and generosity by visiting a local Emirati home through programs like "At the Sheikh Mohammed Centre for Cultural Understanding." Engage in traditional activities like henna painting, Arabic coffee ceremonies, and falconry demonstrations. Take the opportunity to learn about local customs, traditions, and etiquette from Emirati hosts.

Traditional Art and Crafts:
Dubai is a melting pot of art and creativity, and you can find traditional Emirati arts and crafts throughout the city. Visit the Dubai Heritage Village, a living museum that showcases traditional Emirati crafts such as pottery, weaving, and glassblowing. Immerse yourself in workshops and demonstrations to gain insights into the artistic heritage of the region.

Cultural Festivals and Events:
Dubai hosts several cultural festivals and events throughout the year, providing a perfect opportunity to experience traditional Arabic

celebrations. The Dubai Shopping Festival, held annually, offers a glimpse into Emirati culture through traditional music, dance performances, and local crafts. The Dubai Food Festival celebrates the city's diverse culinary scene, showcasing traditional Emirati dishes alongside international cuisines.

Traditional Sports and Entertainment:
Witness traditional Emirati sports like camel racing and falconry, which have been an integral part of Arabic culture for centuries. Attend camel races at Al Marmoom Camel Racetrack and marvel at the speed and agility of these majestic creatures. You can also visit the Dubai Falcon Souk, where you'll find a variety of falcons and learn about the art of falconry.

While Dubai is known for its modernity and futuristic developments, it has successfully preserved and embraced its traditional Arabic culture. By immersing yourself in the heritage, architecture, cuisine, and customs of Dubai, you will gain a deeper appreciation for the city and its roots. Embrace the warmth of Emirati hospitality, explore traditional markets, and participate in cultural events to create lasting memories of your Dubai experience.

CHAPTER SIX

Accommodation Options

•*Luxury Hotels and Resorts*

Dubai, the glittering jewel of the United Arab Emirates, is renowned for its extravagant lifestyle, architectural marvels, and world-class hospitality. As a global hub for luxury and leisure, Dubai boasts an exceptional collection of opulent hotels and resorts that cater to the desires of discerning travelers. This comprehensive Dubai travel guide explores the pinnacle of luxury accommodations, showcasing the city's most iconic and indulgent hotels and resorts.

Burj Al Arab Jumeirah:

Standing tall as an iconic symbol of Dubai's grandeur, the Burj Al Arab Jumeirah is the epitome of luxury. This sail-shaped hotel offers unparalleled opulence with its stunning suite-only accommodations, impeccable personalized service, and breathtaking views of the Arabian Gulf. From the lavish interiors to the world-class restaurants and the renowned Talise Spa, this hotel exceeds all expectations.

Atlantis, The Palm:
Situated on the Palm Jumeirah, Atlantis, The Palm is a mythical paradise that enchants guests with its grandeur. Boasting a magnificent underwater world at the Lost Chambers Aquarium, a thrilling waterpark called Aquaventure, and luxurious suites with mesmerizing ocean views, this resort offers an unforgettable experience. The culinary delights, including celebrity chef restaurants, further elevate the indulgence factor.

Jumeirah Al Qasr:
Nestled within the Madinat Jumeirah complex, Jumeirah Al Qasr exudes Arabian elegance and charm. The palatial rooms and suites, adorned with traditional Middle Eastern elements, provide an oasis of luxury. Guests can enjoy exclusive access to the private beach, indulge in world-class spa treatments, and savor delectable cuisines at the resort's exceptional dining venues.

One&Only The Palm:
A secluded sanctuary on the Palm Jumeirah's western crescent, One&Only The Palm is a tranquil

haven for those seeking privacy and refinement. Its stylish and spacious rooms, adorned with contemporary Arabian flair, offer a serene retreat. Guests can relax in the private pool or indulge in rejuvenating treatments at the Guerlain Spa. The exquisite dining options, including the Michelin-starred STAY by Yannick Alléno, are a gastronomic delight.

Armani Hotel Dubai:
Located in the iconic Burj Khalifa, the world's tallest tower, the Armani Hotel Dubai reflects sophistication and style. The hotel's designer rooms and suites exude elegance, featuring exquisite furnishings and state-of-the-art amenities. With an emphasis on personalized service, guests can experience the epitome of luxury and enjoy access to the Armani/SPA and various fine dining options.

Palazzo Versace Dubai:
Blending Italian elegance with Middle Eastern charm, the Palazzo Versace Dubai offers a truly lavish experience. Inspired by the fashion empire, this hotel boasts opulent interiors, luxurious rooms and suites, and a private marina overlooking the Dubai Creek. Guests can indulge in culinary delights at the hotel's signature restaurants and rejuvenate at the world-class spa.

The Ritz-Carlton, Dubai:
Situated along the pristine shores of the Arabian Gulf, The Ritz-Carlton, Dubai combines timeless luxury with exceptional service. The resort offers spacious and elegant rooms, lush gardens, and a private beach, providing an idyllic retreat. Guests can unwind at the lavish spa, savor gourmet cuisine, and enjoy activities such as golf and tennis.

Bulgari Resort Dubai:
Nestled on Jumeirah Bay Island, the Bulgari Resort Dubai blends Mediterranean charm with Arabian beauty. The resort features lavish villas and mansions with private pools, offering an exclusive retreat. Guests can enjoy the private beach, indulge in holistic treatments at the luxurious spa, and dine at the Michelin-starred Il Ristorante - Niko Romito.

Dubai's luxury hotels and resorts redefine opulence, offering an unparalleled level of service, grandeur, and indulgence. From architectural wonders like the Burj Al Arab Jumeirah to tranquil oases like One&Only The Palm, these properties create unforgettable experiences for discerning travelers. Whether you seek breathtaking views, world-class dining, or rejuvenation at exquisite spas, Dubai's luxury accommodations are sure to cater to your every desire, making your stay in the city an extraordinary and unforgettable one.

•Budget-Friendly Hotels

Dubai, known for its luxurious lifestyle and extravagant experiences, may seem like a destination reserved for the wealthy. However, with careful planning and research, it is possible to find budget-friendly accommodation options that allow travelers to experience the wonders of Dubai without breaking the bank. In this comprehensive travel guide, we will explore some of the best budget-friendly hotels in Dubai, providing you with a range of options that combine affordability with comfort and convenience.

Factors to Consider when Choosing Budget-Friendly Hotels:

Before diving into the specific hotels, it's essential to consider certain factors to ensure you make an informed decision:

a. Location: Dubai is a sprawling city, so choosing a hotel in a convenient location can save both time and transportation costs. Look for hotels near major attractions or close to public transportation.

b. Amenities: While budget-friendly hotels may not offer the same lavish amenities as their upscale counterparts, it's important to find accommodations that provide essential facilities such as comfortable beds, clean rooms, Wi-Fi, and complimentary breakfast.

c. Reviews: Reading reviews from previous guests can provide valuable insights into the quality and service of a hotel. Pay attention to recent reviews to ensure that the hotel maintains its standards.

Budget-Friendly Hotel Recommendations:
Now let's explore some of the best budget-friendly hotels in Dubai, categorized based on their location:
a. Deira:

Citymax Hotel Dubai: Located in the vibrant neighborhood of Deira, Citymax Hotel Dubai offers affordable accommodation with well-furnished rooms, a rooftop pool, and multiple dining options. Its proximity to the metro station and popular attractions like the Dubai Creek and Gold Souk make it an ideal choice for budget-conscious travelers.

Ibis Deira City Centre: Situated adjacent to the City Centre Deira Mall and just a short distance from Dubai International Airport, Ibis Deira City Centre provides comfortable rooms at an affordable price. The hotel offers easy access to the metro station, allowing guests to explore the city conveniently.

b. Bur Dubai:

Arabian Park Hotel: Known for its excellent value for money, Arabian Park Hotel offers spacious rooms, a rooftop swimming pool, and a fitness center. The hotel is located in the Bur Dubai area, close to the Dubai Museum and the historic Al Bastakiya district.

Regent Palace Hotel: Another budget-friendly option in Bur Dubai, Regent Palace Hotel provides comfortable rooms, a rooftop pool, and several dining options. The hotel is within walking distance of the BurJuman Mall and the Dubai Metro station.

c. Dubai Marina:

Premier Inn Dubai Ibn Battuta Mall: Situated near the vibrant Dubai Marina, Premier Inn Dubai Ibn Battuta Mall offers affordable accommodation with modern amenities. The hotel provides easy access to the Ibn Battuta Mall, the Dubai Marina Walk, and the Jumeirah Beach Residence.

Rove Dubai Marina: With its contemporary design and friendly atmosphere, Rove Dubai Marina is a popular choice for budget-conscious travelers. The hotel features comfortable rooms, a 24-hour gym, and a swimming pool. It is conveniently located near the Dubai Marina Mall and Jumeirah Beach Residence.

d. Downtown Dubai:

Ibis Dubai Al Rigga: Situated in Downtown Dubai, Ibis Dubai Al Rigga offers affordable accommodation in close proximity to the iconic Burj Khalifa and Dubai Mall. The hotel provides comfortable rooms, a rooftop swimming pool, and easy access to the Dubai Metro.

Rove Downtown Dubai: Offering stylish and affordable accommodation, Rove Downtown Dubai is an excellent choice for travelers seeking a central location. The hotel features modern rooms, a swimming pool, a 24-hour gym, and is within walking distance of the Burj Khalifa and Dubai Mall.

Dubai's reputation for luxury doesn't mean that budget-conscious travelers cannot enjoy the city's charms. By choosing one of the budget-friendly hotels mentioned in this travel guide, you can experience the wonders of Dubai without compromising on comfort and convenience. Remember to consider factors such as location, amenities, and reviews when making your selection. With careful planning, you can embark on an unforgettable journey in Dubai, even on a limited budget.

•Apartments and Vacation Rentals

As a premier travel destination, Dubai offers a plethora of accommodation options to suit every traveler's needs. In this comprehensive Dubai travel guide, we will explore the world of apartments and vacation rentals, providing valuable insights and tips to help you make the most of your stay in this dazzling city.

The Appeal of Apartments and Vacation Rentals:

1.1 Freedom and Flexibility: Apartments and vacation rentals provide an unparalleled sense of freedom and flexibility, allowing you to live like a local and immerse yourself in the city's charm.

1.2 Cost-Effective: Renting an apartment or vacation home can be a budget-friendly option, especially for families or larger groups, as it often offers more space and amenities at a lower cost than traditional hotels.

1.3 Cultural Immersion: By opting for an apartment or vacation rental, you can experience the local way of life, interact with residents, and explore Dubai's neighborhoods beyond the tourist hotspots.

Popular Neighborhoods for Apartments and Vacation Rentals:

2.1 Downtown Dubai: Located in the heart of the city, Downtown Dubai offers a range of upscale apartments and vacation rentals, providing breathtaking views of iconic landmarks such as the Burj Khalifa and Dubai Fountain.

2.2 Dubai Marina: Known for its stunning waterfront views and a bustling atmosphere, Dubai Marina boasts an array of modern apartments and vacation rentals, with easy access to beaches, restaurants, and entertainment options.

2.3 Jumeirah Beach Residence (JBR): Situated along the picturesque Jumeirah Beach, JBR is a sought-after area for vacation rentals, offering luxurious beachfront apartments and a vibrant community atmosphere.

2.4 Palm Jumeirah: The iconic man-made island of Palm Jumeirah is home to lavish vacation rentals, including beachfront villas and high-end apartments, providing exclusivity and privacy.

Finding the Perfect Apartment or Vacation Rental:

3.1 Online Platforms: Utilize reputable online platforms such as Airbnb, HomeAway, or Booking.com to search for apartments and vacation rentals in Dubai. These platforms offer a wide range of options, allowing you to filter based on location, amenities, and budget.

3.2 Considerations: When selecting an apartment or vacation rental, factors such as size, number of bedrooms, amenities (pool, gym, parking), proximity to attractions, and public transportation options should be taken into account.

3.3 Booking in Advance: Dubai is a popular tourist destination, so it is advisable to book your apartment or vacation rental well in advance to secure the best options and avoid disappointment during peak travel seasons.

Apartment and Vacation Rental Amenities:
4.1 Fully Equipped Kitchens: Many apartments and vacation rentals in Dubai come with fully equipped kitchens, allowing you to prepare your own meals and save on dining expenses.

4.2 Shared Facilities: Some rentals offer shared facilities like swimming pools, fitness centers, and communal lounges, adding value to your stay.

4.3 Concierge Services: Several high-end vacation rentals provide dedicated concierge services to assist with various needs, including booking tours, restaurant reservations, and transportation arrangements.

Local Regulations and Tips:
5.1 Vacation Rental Regulations: Familiarize yourself with Dubai's vacation rental regulations to ensure compliance and avoid any legal issues during your stay.

5.2 Tourist Dirham Fee: Keep in mind that Dubai imposes a nightly "Tourist Dirham" fee, which is typically collected by the accommodation provider upon check-in. This fee contributes to the city's tourism infrastructure.

5.3 Security Deposits: Some apartment and vacation rental providers may require a security deposit, which is refundable upon check-out, provided there is no damage to the property.

5.4 Respect Local Customs: Dubai has a rich cultural heritage, and it is important to respect local customs, such as dress codes and social norms, especially in residential areas.

Additional Tips for a Memorable Stay:

6.1 Transportation: Dubai has an efficient public transportation system, including metro, buses, and taxis. Familiarize yourself with these options to explore the city conveniently from your apartment or vacation rental.

6.2 Essential Supplies: Upon arrival, stock up on essential supplies such as groceries, toiletries, and drinking water to ensure a comfortable stay.

6.3 Explore Neighborhoods: Venture beyond your immediate surroundings and explore different neighborhoods in Dubai to experience the city's diversity, from historic areas like Al Fahidi to modern districts like Dubai Design District (d3).

6.4 Local Experiences: Engage in activities like desert safaris, visiting traditional souks, and enjoying authentic Emirati cuisine to truly immerse yourself in the local culture.

Choosing an apartment or vacation rental in Dubai offers a unique opportunity to embrace the city's captivating charm and live like a local. With its wide range of options and attractive neighborhoods, Dubai ensures a memorable and authentic travel experience. By considering the provided insights and tips, you can make informed decisions when selecting an apartment or vacation rental, setting the stage for an unforgettable journey in this dazzling metropolis.

•Unique Accommodation Experiences

Dubai, the crown jewel of the United Arab Emirates, is renowned for its unparalleled opulence, architectural marvels, and extravagant lifestyle. While the city is synonymous with grandeur and luxury, it also offers unique accommodation experiences that go beyond the ordinary. From awe-inspiring, world-class hotels to mesmerizing desert retreats and innovative underwater suites, Dubai presents travelers with a remarkable range of choices to create unforgettable memories. In this Dubai travel guide, we will explore some of the most unique accommodation experiences that embody the city's spirit of luxury and offer an unparalleled level of comfort and indulgence.

Iconic Landmark Hotels
Dubai is home to some of the world's most iconic hotels, which have become synonymous with the city's grandeur. The Burj Al Arab, often referred to as the world's only seven-star hotel, stands tall as an architectural masterpiece. Its opulent suites and personalized service redefine luxury, making it an exceptional choice for discerning travelers. Another remarkable landmark is the sail-shaped Burj Khalifa, the world's tallest building, which houses the Armani Hotel. Blending elegance with contemporary design, the hotel offers stunning

views of the city and an array of exceptional amenities.

Desert Retreats

For those seeking a unique and immersive experience, Dubai's desert retreats provide an oasis of tranquility amidst the vast golden dunes. Resorts like Bab Al Shams Desert Resort and Spa offer a magical escape, combining traditional Arabian hospitality with modern comforts. Guests can indulge in camel rides, sandboarding, and desert safaris, followed by evenings filled with traditional music, belly dancing, and delicious Arabian cuisine. The luxurious tented accommodations provide an authentic Bedouin experience, allowing guests to unwind under the starlit desert sky.

Innovative Underwater Suites

Dubai is a city that continually pushes the boundaries of innovation and imagination, as exemplified by its underwater accommodations. The Atlantis, The Palm hotel offers the unique opportunity to stay in an underwater suite, known as the Neptune and Poseidon Underwater Suites. These exquisite suites boast floor-to-ceiling windows that showcase the vibrant marine life of the Ambassador Lagoon. Guests can sleep surrounded by the captivating beauty of the underwater world, making for an extraordinary and unforgettable experience.

Floating Hotels and Resorts
Dubai's stunning coastline and iconic man-made islands, such as Palm Jumeirah, have given rise to another extraordinary accommodation option – floating hotels and resorts. The World Islands, a collection of artificial islands shaped like a world map, is home to the floating Zaya Nurai Island Resort. This secluded paradise offers luxurious villas with private pools, direct beach access, and stunning views of the Arabian Gulf. Floating hotels like the Queen Elizabeth 2 (QE2) provide a unique blend of maritime heritage and contemporary luxury, as guests get the chance to stay aboard a legendary ocean liner.

Lavish Desert Glamping
For those seeking a more adventurous yet lavish experience, Dubai offers an intriguing combination of desert and glamping. Resorts like Al Maha, a Luxury Collection Desert Resort and Spa, redefine the concept of glamping by offering sumptuous tented suites with private pools, sun decks, and breathtaking views of the desert landscape. Guests can enjoy wildlife safaris, falconry displays, and spa

treatments inspired by local traditions, creating an unforgettable blend of luxury and natural beauty.

Dubai's unique accommodation experiences reflect the city's ambition to offer extraordinary and unforgettable stays for every traveler. From the iconic landmark hotels that epitomize grandeur to the floating resorts and underwater suites that showcase innovation and imagination, Dubai's hospitality industry continuously raises the bar. Desert retreats and luxurious glamping experiences provide an authentic taste of Arabian culture, offering tranquility amidst the vast dunes and starlit nights. Each accommodation option in Dubai guarantees world-class service, exquisite design, and a captivating atmosphere that leaves an indelible mark on every visitor.

When visiting Dubai, travelers have the opportunity to immerse themselves in an exceptional blend of luxury, comfort, and unparalleled experiences. Whether exploring the architectural wonders of the city or venturing into the enchanting desert, these unique accommodation choices ensure that every moment spent in Dubai is an extraordinary journey that lingers in the memory long after the visit concludes.

CHAPTER SEVEN

Cultural Experiences

•*Dubai Opera House*

Dubai, the jewel of the United Arab Emirates, has long been renowned for its modern architecture, luxurious lifestyle, and innovative attractions. Among its many iconic landmarks, the Dubai Opera House stands out as a testament to the city's commitment to the arts and culture. This magnificent venue has become a cultural hub, hosting world-class performances that mesmerize visitors from around the globe. In this travel guide, we will explore the Dubai Opera House, its architectural marvels, the diverse range of performances it offers, and the overall experiences that await those who visit this captivating venue.

I. A Glimpse into Dubai Opera House
The Dubai Opera House, located in the vibrant downtown area, is a stunning architectural

masterpiece that perfectly combines contemporary design with traditional Arabic elements. Designed in the shape of a dhow, a traditional Arabian sailing vessel, the building's sleek curves and iconic glass façade make it a sight to behold. The interior is equally impressive, featuring a spacious auditorium with a seating capacity of 2,000, state-of-the-art acoustics, and a flexible stage capable of accommodating various productions.

II. *A World of Performances*

The Dubai Opera House offers a diverse range of performances that cater to all artistic tastes. From classical music concerts and ballets to opera, theater, and contemporary dance shows, there is something for everyone. Internationally acclaimed artists, ensembles, and troupes grace the stage, ensuring an unforgettable experience for culture enthusiasts.

a) Classical Music and Opera: The Dubai Opera House frequently hosts renowned symphony orchestras, opera companies, and soloists. Audiences can revel in the beauty of classical compositions or indulge in an operatic masterpiece, enjoying the enchanting atmosphere and extraordinary acoustics of the venue.

b) Theater and Musicals: Broadway hits, West End productions, and locally produced theatrical performances delight theater lovers at the Dubai Opera House. Audiences can witness captivating storytelling, impressive sets, and stellar performances, immersing themselves in the world of drama and musical theater.

c) Dance and Contemporary Performances: World-class dance companies showcase their talent through captivating performances that blend tradition and innovation. From classical ballet to contemporary dance, the Dubai Opera House offers a platform for both renowned and emerging artists to leave audiences spellbound.

III. *Beyond the Performances*
Apart from the mesmerizing performances, the Dubai Opera House offers a host of other experiences that enhance visitors' cultural journey.

a) Guided Tours: Visitors can take guided tours of the venue to gain insights into its architectural wonders, learn about the building's history, and explore the backstage area. These tours offer a behind-the-scenes glimpse into the world of theater and opera.

b) Culinary Delights: The Dubai Opera House boasts a selection of restaurants and cafes, allowing visitors to savor delectable cuisines before or after the performances. From elegant fine dining establishments to casual eateries, there are options to suit every taste.

c) Cultural Events: In addition to performances, the Dubai Opera House hosts cultural events such as art exhibitions, film screenings, and educational workshops. These events provide an immersive experience, allowing visitors to engage with various art forms and learn about different cultures.

IV. Practical Information
a) Tickets and Reservations: It is advisable to book tickets in advance, especially for popular performances. Tickets can be purchased online or at the box office. Prices vary depending on the performance and seating category.

b) Dress Code: The Dubai Opera House follows a smart-casual dress code. While there is no strict requirement, it is recommended to dress modestly and elegantly, particularly for opera and ballet performances.

c) Accessibility: The venue is designed to be accessible to all visitors, with wheelchair ramps, designated seating, and other facilities to accommodate individuals with disabilities. It is advisable to inform the staff in advance for any special requirements.

Dubai Opera House stands as a beacon of culture and art, offering visitors an extraordinary journey through the performing arts. From its breathtaking architecture to the world-class performances, this venue captures the essence of Dubai's commitment to innovation, luxury, and cultural enrichment. Whether you are a music aficionado, theater lover, or simply seeking a unique experience, a visit to the Dubai Opera House promises to be an unforgettable highlight of your Dubai itinerary. So, immerse yourself in the magic of the performing arts and witness the splendor of this cultural marvel in the heart of the city.

•*Dubai Art Galleries*

Dubai, known as a bustling metropolis and a global hub for business and luxury, has also emerged as a vibrant center for art and culture. With its thriving art scene, the city boasts a multitude of world-class art galleries that showcase diverse artistic expressions from both local and international artists. In this Dubai travel guide, we will delve into the fascinating realm of Dubai art galleries, offering you a glimpse into the city's creative spirit and providing recommendations for art enthusiasts and curious travelers alike.

The Rise of Dubai's Art Scene

Dubai's rapid development as a cultural destination has been instrumental in nurturing its art scene. In recent years, the city has actively sought to establish itself as a global hub for art, attracting artists, collectors, and art enthusiasts from around the world. The government's efforts in promoting cultural initiatives and hosting prestigious events, such as Art Dubai, have played a pivotal role in transforming the city's landscape into a flourishing haven for art.

Exploring Prominent Art Galleries in Dubai

2.1 The Third Line

Located in Alserkal Avenue, The Third Line is a contemporary art gallery known for its innovative exhibitions. With a focus on artists from the Middle East and North Africa, this gallery offers a platform for thought-provoking and socially engaged artworks. Visitors can explore a diverse range of mediums, including painting, sculpture, photography, and video installations.

2.2 Gallery Isabelle van den Eynde
Situated in Alserkal Avenue, Gallery Isabelle van den Eynde showcases contemporary art from the Middle East and beyond. The gallery represents a roster of talented artists who engage with various artistic practices, challenging conventions and exploring themes deeply rooted in the region's cultural identity.

2.3 Cuadro Fine Art Gallery
Cuadro Fine Art Gallery, located in the Dubai International Financial Centre (DIFC), is a prominent space dedicated to modern and contemporary art. It features exhibitions by established international artists, as well as emerging talents. The gallery's diverse program spans different art movements and styles, offering visitors a comprehensive perspective on contemporary art.

2.4 Meem Gallery
Meem Gallery, situated in Al Quoz, specializes in modern and contemporary art from the Arab world.

The gallery showcases works by renowned artists, emphasizing the cultural significance and artistic contributions of the region. Meem Gallery's collection reflects the rich heritage and evolving narratives of Arab art.

2.5 Alserkal Avenue Galleries
Alserkal Avenue is a dynamic arts district housing multiple art galleries, creative spaces, and cultural organizations. It serves as a vibrant platform for artists, curators, and collectors, showcasing a range of contemporary artworks and hosting engaging exhibitions throughout the year. Some noteworthy galleries within Alserkal Avenue include Carbon 12, Ayyam Gallery, and Green Art Gallery.

Art Events and Festivals
Dubai's art scene comes alive with an array of events and festivals that celebrate artistic expression. One of the most prominent events is Art Dubai, an annual international art fair that brings together galleries, artists, and collectors from around the world. Art Dubai features a diverse program of exhibitions, talks, and performances, offering a comprehensive overview of the global art market.
In addition to Art Dubai, Dubai Art Season is a month-long celebration of arts and culture,

encompassing various events and activities such as gallery exhibitions, public installations, and workshops. This city-wide initiative highlights the city's commitment to fostering creativity and engaging the community.

Supporting Local Artists
Dubai's art galleries actively support and promote local artists, providing a platform for emerging talents to showcase their work. Many galleries collaborate with local artists through exhibitions, residencies, and mentoring programs, fostering a sense of community and nurturing artistic growth. These initiatives have contributed to the development of a strong local art scene and have helped elevate the status of Dubai as a cultural destination.

Dubai's art galleries offer an immersive experience into the city's dynamic art scene, providing visitors with a diverse range of artistic expressions and cultural perspectives. From contemporary art to traditional forms, Dubai's galleries showcase the richness and diversity of global art. Whether you're an art enthusiast or a curious traveler, exploring these galleries will undoubtedly enrich your understanding of Dubai's cultural landscape. So, step into the vibrant world of Dubai art galleries and uncover the creativity that thrives within this cosmopolitan city.

•Heritage and Cultural Tours

Dubai, the gleaming gem of the United Arab Emirates, is widely renowned for its modern skyscrapers, luxurious resorts, and extravagant shopping malls. However, beyond its cosmopolitan façade, Dubai boasts a captivating heritage and a diverse cultural tapestry that dates back centuries. In this comprehensive Dubai travel guide, we delve into the city's rich heritage and cultural tours, unveiling the hidden treasures and immersive experiences that showcase Dubai's vibrant past and present. From ancient historical sites to traditional souks and art districts, Dubai offers a plethora of opportunities for travelers seeking an authentic cultural encounter.

Unveiling the Historical Sites:

Dubai's history stretches back thousands of years, and exploring its historical sites provides a glimpse into the city's fascinating past. Start your heritage tour at Al Fahidi Historic District, the oldest neighborhood in Dubai, where beautifully preserved wind-tower houses, now transformed into museums and art galleries, showcase traditional Emirati architecture. Don't miss the Dubai Museum, located within the historic Al Fahidi Fort, which narrates the city's transformation from a humble fishing village to a global metropolis.

Embracing Traditional Souks:

To truly immerse yourself in Dubai's cultural fabric, visit the traditional souks that have stood as bustling marketplaces for centuries. Begin with a trip to the Deira Spice Souk, where you'll encounter a vibrant array of aromatic spices, herbs, and traditional perfumes. Continue your journey to the nearby Gold Souk, an awe-inspiring spectacle of glittering gold jewelry, offering an opportunity to admire the traditional craftsmanship of the region.

Appreciating Islamic Architecture:

Dubai is home to several remarkable examples of Islamic architecture, each exuding splendor and grandeur. The Jumeirah Mosque, an iconic landmark, offers guided tours for non-Muslims, providing insights into Islamic traditions and beliefs. Another architectural marvel is the stunning Al Farooq Omar Bin Al Khattab Mosque, showcasing the fusion of traditional and modern architectural elements.

Dubai's Cultural Centers:
To gain a deeper understanding of Dubai's cultural heritage, visit the city's cultural centers that promote art, music, and traditional performances. The Dubai Opera is a world-class venue hosting a variety of performances, including ballet, opera, and theatrical productions. For a taste of traditional Emirati arts and crafts, head to the Sheikh Mohammed Centre for Cultural Understanding, where workshops and interactive sessions allow visitors to learn about local traditions, henna painting, and Arabic calligraphy.

Exploring Heritage Villages:
Dubai's Heritage Villages transport visitors back in time to experience the traditional Bedouin way of life. Hatta Heritage Village, nestled in the Hajar Mountains, offers a glimpse into the region's pre-oil era, with restored buildings, ancient artifacts, and traditional cultural exhibits. Another captivating destination is the Sheikh Mohammed Centre for

Cultural Understanding's Heritage House in Al Bastakiya, where visitors can explore a well-preserved traditional Emirati house and learn about the customs and traditions of the past.

Alserkal Avenue: Dubai's Art District:

For art enthusiasts, a visit to Alserkal Avenue, Dubai's vibrant art district, is a must. Formerly an industrial area, Alserkal Avenue has transformed into a hub for contemporary art, design, and culture. Explore the numerous galleries, art spaces, and creative studios that showcase local and international talent. The district also hosts art exhibitions, cultural events, and workshops, providing a dynamic platform for artistic exchange.

Al Fahidi Street and Meena Bazaar:

Venture into Al Fahidi Street and Meena Bazaar, bustling commercial areas where you'll find an amalgamation of cultures and a plethora of traditional shops. From vibrant textiles and fabrics to exquisite handcrafted items, these vibrant streets offer an ideal setting for shopping and experiencing the local culture. Indulge in a traditional Emirati meal at one of the local eateries, savoring authentic flavors and culinary traditions.

Dubai's heritage and cultural tours provide a captivating journey through time, revealing the city's deep-rooted traditions and rich historical tapestry. From exploring ancient historical sites to immersing oneself in traditional souks and embracing Islamic architecture, Dubai offers a wealth of cultural experiences. By visiting cultural centers, heritage villages, and the vibrant art district, travelers can gain a comprehensive understanding of Dubai's diverse cultural landscape. So, embark on a journey of discovery, and let Dubai's rich heritage and cultural tours weave their magic, leaving you with cherished memories and a profound appreciation for this dynamic city.

•*Traditional Arabic Music and Dance*

Dubai, a vibrant and cosmopolitan city, offers a captivating blend of modernity and tradition. Amidst the towering skyscrapers and luxurious shopping malls, Dubai also harbors a rich cultural heritage deeply rooted in the region's history. Traditional Arabic music and dance are integral components of Emirati culture, providing a gateway to the city's enchanting past. In this travel guide, we will delve into the world of Traditional Arabic Music and Dance in Dubai, exploring the captivating rhythms, captivating melodies, and graceful movements that have shaped the cultural landscape of this magnificent city.

I. *Traditional Arabic Music :*

Origins and Influences:
Traditional Arabic music traces its roots back centuries and has been influenced by diverse cultures across the Middle East, North Africa, and even further afield. It has its foundations in the Islamic traditions and the Arab maqam system, a unique melodic structure.

Instruments:
a) Oud: The oud, a stringed instrument similar to a lute, is considered the king of traditional Arabic music. Its rich, resonant sound is often the focal point of musical performances.
b) Nay: The nay, a reed flute, produces hauntingly beautiful melodies and is frequently used in Arabic ensembles.

c) Qanun: A plucked string instrument, the qanun adds a melodic layer to the music, providing depth and harmony.
d) Percussion Instruments: Drums like the darbuka and the riqq, as well as finger cymbals called sagat, contribute to the rhythmic foundation of traditional Arabic music.

Genres:
Arabic music encompasses a wide array of genres, each with its distinct characteristics. The most notable genres include:
a) Tarab: Known for its emotional and introspective nature, tarab music elicits deep feelings and a sense of nostalgia.
b) Sama'i: Derived from the Ottoman classical tradition, sama'i features intricate rhythms and evocative melodies.
c) Dabke: A lively folk music genre often accompanied by line dancing, dabke is popular in celebratory events and weddings.

Venues and Performances:
Visitors to Dubai can immerse themselves in the enchanting sounds of traditional Arabic music by attending performances at various venues. The Dubai Opera, Al Majaz Amphitheatre, and cultural

centers like the Alserkal Avenue host concerts and events showcasing talented musicians and singers.

II. Traditional Arabic Dance :

Overview and Styles:
Traditional Arabic dance, or raqs sharqi, is a mesmerizing art form that combines graceful movements, expressive gestures, and intricate footwork. It has evolved over centuries and encompasses several distinct styles, including:
a) Belly Dance: The most famous and widely recognized Arabic dance style, belly dance, showcases the dancer's skill in isolating different parts of the body and fluid hip movements.

b) Debke: As mentioned earlier, debke is not only a folk music genre but also a line dance. It involves synchronized footwork and energetic movements, often performed in a group.

c) Tanoura: Originating from Egypt, tanoura features a male dancer twirling in a colorful skirt, symbolizing spiritual enlightenment and joy.

d) Saidi: Hailing from Upper Egypt, saidi is characterized by its lively and energetic movements, incorporating the use of a stick or cane.

Traditional Dance Costumes:
Traditional Arabic dance costumes are vibrant and ornate, reflecting the cultural heritage of the region. Women often wear bedlah, which consists of a sequined bra, a heavily embellished belt, a flowing skirt, and accessories such as veils or headdresses. Men don traditional attire such as a thobe (long shirt) and a head covering like a ghutra or shemagh.

Dance Performances and Events:
Dubai showcases traditional Arabic dance through various performances and events. The Dubai Mall, Global Village, and cultural festivals like the Dubai Shopping Festival and Dubai Summer Surprises often feature dance shows where visitors can witness the captivating beauty of Arabic dance firsthand.

Dubai, with its thriving multicultural landscape, offers a remarkable window into the world of Traditional Arabic Music and Dance. Exploring the diverse genres, enchanting melodies, and captivating dance styles allows visitors to immerse themselves in the rich cultural tapestry of this vibrant city. From attending mesmerizing concerts to witnessing the hypnotic movements of traditional Arabic dance, Dubai provides an unforgettable experience where ancient traditions come to life. Whether you are an avid music lover or a curious traveler seeking to embrace the local culture, the traditional Arabic music and dance scene in Dubai will undoubtedly leave you with lasting memories and a deeper appreciation for the city's cultural heritage.

•*Al Fahidi Historic District*

Dubai, known for its ultramodern skyscrapers and luxurious resorts, also boasts a hidden gem that offers a glimpse into its rich cultural heritage: the Al Fahidi Historic District. Nestled in the heart of Old Dubai, this charming neighborhood takes visitors on a journey back in time, allowing them to immerse themselves in the city's history and traditions. In this comprehensive travel guide, we will delve into the captivating story of Al Fahidi Historic District, highlighting its key attractions, cultural experiences, and practical tips for an unforgettable visit.

Historical Background:

Al Fahidi Historic District, formerly known as Bastakiya, dates back to the late 19th century. Established by wealthy Persian merchants, the neighborhood was a thriving trading hub renowned for its wind-tower houses and traditional architecture. In the 1980s, recognizing the significance of this historical area, the Dubai government embarked on a restoration project to preserve its heritage, transforming it into the charming district it is today.

Getting There:
Al Fahidi Historic District is conveniently located in the Bur Dubai area, just a short distance from Dubai Creek and the Dubai Museum. Visitors can reach the district by various means of transportation, including taxis, public buses, or the Dubai Metro (alight at Al Fahidi Metro Station). For a more scenic experience, consider taking an abra (traditional wooden boat) ride across Dubai Creek.

Exploring the District:
As you step into Al Fahidi Historic District, you'll be transported to a bygone era characterized by narrow alleyways, traditional courtyard houses, and wind-tower architecture. Here are some of the must-visit attractions and activities within the district:

3.1. Dubai Museum:
Start your journey at the Dubai Museum, housed within the 18th-century Al Fahidi Fort. This captivating museum showcases Dubai's transformation from a humble fishing village to a global metropolis through a fascinating collection of artifacts, dioramas, and interactive exhibits.

3.2. Cultural Centers and Museums:
Within Al Fahidi Historic District, you'll find several cultural centers and museums that offer a deeper understanding of Emirati heritage. The Sheikh Mohammed Centre for Cultural Understanding provides insightful tours and activities, including traditional Emirati meals, where visitors can engage with locals and learn about their customs and traditions. The Coin Museum and Coffee Museum are also worth exploring to delve into the region's historical and cultural roots.

3.3. Art Galleries:
Art enthusiasts will appreciate the vibrant art scene in Al Fahidi Historic District. The neighborhood is home to numerous art galleries that showcase local and international talents. From contemporary art to

traditional calligraphy, these galleries offer a diverse range of artistic expressions.

3.4. Heritage Houses:
One of the highlights of Al Fahidi Historic District is the opportunity to visit well-preserved heritage houses. Step into the past as you explore the charming courtyard houses with their traditional wind towers. Many of these houses have been converted into art galleries, boutique hotels, and cultural spaces, allowing visitors to experience the essence of Old Dubai.

Cultural Experiences:
To truly immerse yourself in the local culture, make sure to partake in the following experiences within Al Fahidi Historic District:

4.1. Arabic Calligraphy:
Enroll in a calligraphy workshop and learn the art of Arabic calligraphy, a cherished tradition in the region. Skilled instructors will guide you through the intricate techniques and history of this beautiful script.

4.2. Traditional Crafts:
Discover the craftsmanship of Emirati artisans by participating in workshops that teach traditional crafts such as pottery, weaving, and embroidery.

These hands-on experiences offer insights into the skill and creativity that have shaped the local culture.

4.3. Heritage Tours:
Embark on a guided heritage tour of Al Fahidi Historic District to gain a deeper understanding of its historical significance. Local guides share captivating stories and anecdotes, taking you on a journey through the district's past and present.

Dining and Refreshments:
Al Fahidi Historic District offers a range of culinary delights that cater to various tastes. From traditional Emirati cuisine to international flavors, here are a few dining options to consider:

5.1. Arabian Tea House:
Located in a restored wind-tower house, the Arabian Tea House is a popular spot to indulge in Emirati cuisine. Savor traditional dishes such as machboos (spiced rice with meat or fish) and luqaimat (sweet dumplings), all while enjoying the serene courtyard setting.

5.2. Local Cafés:
The district is dotted with charming local cafés where you can unwind and enjoy a cup of aromatic Arabic coffee or refreshing mint lemonade. These

cozy establishments often offer outdoor seating, providing a perfect vantage point to observe the district's bustling atmosphere.

Practical Tips:
To make the most of your visit to Al Fahidi Historic District, keep these practical tips in mind:
6.1. Dress Code:
Dubai follows a modest dress code, especially in its heritage areas. It is advisable to dress respectfully, covering shoulders and knees, to show cultural sensitivity.

6.2. Timings and Admission:
Most attractions within the district are open from 9:00 AM to 6:00 PM, with slight variations. The Dubai Museum is closed on Fridays. Admission fees for attractions are generally affordable, with discounts for students and children.

6.3. Exploring on Foot:
The best way to explore Al Fahidi Historic District is on foot. Wear comfortable shoes, as you will be navigating narrow alleyways and uneven surfaces.

6.4. Weather Considerations:
Dubai experiences hot temperatures, especially during the summer months. It is advisable to visit

early in the day or during the cooler months to enjoy your time in the district comfortably.

Al Fahidi Historic District in Dubai is a testament to the city's commitment to preserving its cultural heritage. By immersing yourself in the historical charm of this district, you'll gain a deeper appreciation for Dubai's evolution from a humble trading port to a cosmopolitan city. From its captivating museums and art galleries to its traditional houses and cultural experiences, Al Fahidi Historic District offers an enriching journey through time, leaving visitors with lasting memories of Old Dubai's vibrant past.

•*Dubai Miracle Garden*

Dubai Miracle Garden is an awe-inspiring horticultural masterpiece nestled in the heart of Dubai, captivating visitors with its vibrant floral displays and enchanting landscapes. Spanning over 72,000 square meters, this botanical paradise is a testament to Dubai's remarkable vision and engineering prowess. With its exquisite flower arrangements, unique attractions, and delightful ambience, Dubai Miracle Garden offers an unforgettable experience for nature lovers, families, and tourists seeking a resplendent escape from the bustling city. In this comprehensive Dubai travel guide, we will explore the wonders of Dubai Miracle Garden, from its inception to its must-see attractions and practical information for an immersive visit.

I. History and Creation of Dubai Miracle Garden :

Dubai Miracle Garden emerged from the visionary ideas of the Akar Landscaping and Agriculture Company, a renowned landscape and design firm in the United Arab Emirates. It was opened to the public in February 2013 as the world's largest natural flower garden, surpassing 45 million flowers across various species and varieties.

The garden's creation required ingenious engineering and technical expertise, considering Dubai's arid climate and limited water resources. Innovative irrigation systems were employed, utilizing treated wastewater for sustainable plant growth. The result was a magnificent oasis of vibrant colors, breath-taking structures, and intricate designs that mesmerize visitors from around the globe.

II. A Floral Wonderland: Key Attractions :

a. The Flower Avenue:
As visitors enter Dubai Miracle Garden, they are welcomed by the enchanting Flower Avenue, a 1-kilometer pathway adorned with a canopy of colorful umbrellas. This captivating sight provides a delightful introduction to the garden's splendor.

b. The Emirates A380 Display:
Dubai Miracle Garden is famous for its larger-than-life floral structures, and one of the most iconic is the Emirates A380 display. It showcases a replica of the world's largest passenger aircraft, the Airbus A380, meticulously crafted using flowers and plants. This captivating creation is a testament to Dubai's grandeur and attention to detail.

c. Heart Passage:
The Heart Passage is another extraordinary attraction, featuring a heart-shaped pathway adorned with millions of blooming flowers. It provides the perfect backdrop for romantic walks and memorable photographs.

d. Butterfly Garden:
Adjacent to Dubai Miracle Garden, the Butterfly Garden is a serene sanctuary where visitors can witness the graceful fluttering of hundreds of butterfly species. The garden's lush greenery and colorful blooms create an ideal habitat for these delicate creatures, offering a mesmerizing experience for nature enthusiasts.

e. Disney Avenue:
For families and children, the Disney Avenue is a whimsical section of Dubai Miracle Garden that brings beloved Disney characters to life through meticulously designed topiaries. From Mickey Mouse to Snow White, visitors can explore a magical world filled with their favorite characters.

f. Floral Clock:
The enchanting Floral Clock is an impressive timepiece comprising countless blooms, meticulously arranged to form the shape of a clock. This floral masterpiece is not only a visual spectacle but also a functional timekeeping device.

g. Lake Park:
The Lake Park within Dubai Miracle Garden is an oasis of tranquility, featuring stunning floral arrangements surrounding a picturesque lake.

Visitors can relax on the benches, take leisurely strolls, or rent a pedal boat to explore the serene waters.

III. Practical Information and Tips for Visitors :

a. Opening Hours and Seasons:

Dubai Miracle Garden is generally open from October to April, as the extreme summer temperatures are not conducive to the garden's delicate floral displays. The opening hours are typically from 9 am to 9 pm on weekdays, and extended hours on weekends and public holidays.

b. Ticketing and Entrance Fees:

Entrance fees to Dubai Miracle Garden are reasonable, and children under the age of three can enter for free. It is advisable to purchase tickets in advance to avoid long queues, especially during peak visiting times.

c. Accessibility and Transportation:

The garden is located in Dubailand, approximately 25 minutes away from Dubai's city center. Visitors can easily reach Dubai Miracle Garden by private car, taxi, or using public transportation. Various tour operators also offer guided tours that include transportation to and from the garden.

d. Dress Code and Amenities:
Dubai Miracle Garden is an outdoor attraction, so it is recommended to dress comfortably and wear sunscreen to protect against the sun. The garden provides amenities such as restrooms, cafes, and seating areas for visitors' convenience.

e. Photography and Etiquette:
Photography is encouraged in Dubai Miracle Garden, as it offers countless picture-perfect moments. However, it is important to be respectful of the surroundings and other visitors while capturing memories. Trampling or picking flowers is strictly prohibited.

IV. Future Developments and Sustainability Initiatives :
Dubai Miracle Garden continues to evolve and innovate, constantly adding new attractions and expanding its floral wonders. The garden's management is committed to sustainability and employs various initiatives to reduce its ecological footprint. These include water recycling, using renewable energy sources, and promoting environmental awareness among visitors.

Dubai Miracle Garden is an extraordinary testament to Dubai's ambition and creativity. It has transformed a desert landscape into a blossoming oasis, captivating visitors with its awe-inspiring floral displays and enchanting attractions. From the larger-than-life floral structures to the serene Butterfly Garden, Dubai Miracle Garden offers a sensory feast for nature lovers and a delightful experience for families and tourists alike. A visit to this remarkable horticultural paradise is sure to leave a lasting impression and create cherished memories of Dubai's unique blend of innovation and natural beauty.

Dubai Global Village

Dubai, the jewel of the United Arab Emirates (UAE), is renowned for its stunning architecture, luxury shopping, and vibrant culture. Among its many attractions, Dubai Global Village stands out as a unique and captivating destination. This travel guide will provide a comprehensive overview of Dubai Global Village, including its history, attractions, entertainment options, dining experiences, and practical tips for visitors.

History and Overview:
Dubai Global Village was established in 1996 and has since become a significant cultural and entertainment landmark in the region. It is an annual multicultural festival, typically open from November to April, showcasing the diverse traditions, cuisines, and crafts from around the world. Spanning over 1.6 million square feet, the village offers a fusion of entertainment, shopping, and culinary delights.

Attractions:
a. Pavilions and Exhibitions:
Dubai Global Village is divided into pavilions representing various countries and regions. Each pavilion showcases their unique culture, architecture, and traditional handicrafts. Visitors can explore pavilions from over 90 countries, such as Egypt, India, China, Saudi Arabia, Morocco, and more. These exhibits offer a chance to immerse oneself in the vibrant cultures and traditions of different nations.

b. Entertainment Shows:

The village hosts a wide array of captivating live performances throughout the season. Visitors can enjoy cultural dances, musical concerts, acrobatic acts, and theatrical productions from talented artists representing different cultures. These performances provide an enchanting and immersive experience, leaving visitors enthralled.

c. Funfair and Rides:
For thrill-seekers and families, Dubai Global Village offers a lively funfair with exciting rides and games. From Ferris wheels to roller coasters, bumper cars to merry-go-rounds, there are attractions for visitors of all ages. The funfair creates a lively atmosphere, filled with laughter and excitement.

d. Fireworks:
As the night falls, Dubai Global Village comes alive with spectacular firework displays that light up the sky. The dazzling colors and patterns create a breathtaking backdrop, adding a touch of magic to the village's ambiance. These nightly fireworks are a must-see spectacle for visitors.

Shopping Experience:
Dubai Global Village is a shopper's paradise, offering an extensive range of products from around the world. Visitors can explore numerous

market stalls and kiosks, each offering unique handicrafts, clothing, jewelry, and souvenirs. It provides an opportunity to shop for exquisite items and unique gifts while immersing oneself in the cultural diversity of the global marketplace.

Culinary Delights:
Food enthusiasts will be delighted by the wide variety of culinary options available at Dubai Global Village. The food stalls and restaurants offer an extensive range of international cuisines, allowing visitors to savor flavors from every corner of the globe. From traditional Arabic delicacies to Asian street food, European delights to African specialties, there is something to satisfy every palate.

Practical Tips for Visitors:
a. Timing and Tickets:
Dubai Global Village operates from November to April each year, and it is advisable to check the specific dates before planning a visit. Visitors can purchase tickets online or at the entrance. It is recommended to arrive early to make the most of the day and avoid long queues.

b. Comfortable Attire and Footwear:

As Dubai Global Village covers a vast area, comfortable attire and footwear are essential for an enjoyable experience. The village is an outdoor venue, so wearing lightweight and breathable clothing is advisable, especially during the warmer months.

c. Transportation:
Dubai Global Village is located on Sheikh Mohammed Bin Zayed Road (E311), and various transportation options are available. Visitors can opt for taxis, private cars, or use public transportation services like the Dubai Metro and buses. Adequate parking facilities are also available for those driving their vehicles.

d. Plan Ahead:
Given the size of Dubai Global Village and the multitude of attractions, it is beneficial to plan the visit in advance. Checking the event schedule, shows, and performances can help prioritize the must-see experiences and make the most of the visit.

Dubai Global Village is a captivating and vibrant destination that encapsulates the spirit of multiculturalism and global unity. With its diverse pavilions, live performances, exhilarating rides, and tantalizing cuisines, it offers an unforgettable experience for visitors. Exploring the village allows one to embark on a cultural journey around the world without leaving Dubai. Whether shopping for unique souvenirs, indulging in delicious global cuisines, or immersing oneself in the rich traditions of different countries, Dubai Global Village is a must-visit destination that embodies the cosmopolitan charm of this remarkable city.

•Dubai Frame

Dubai, the crown jewel of the United Arab Emirates, is renowned for its groundbreaking architecture and iconic landmarks. Among these landmarks is the Dubai Frame, an awe-inspiring architectural marvel that offers visitors a unique and breathtaking experience. Standing tall in Zabeel Park, the Dubai Frame captures the essence of Dubai's past, present, and future, showcasing the city's rapid growth and transformation. This travel guide aims to provide comprehensive insights into the Dubai Frame, highlighting its history, design, attractions, and practical information to ensure an unforgettable visit to this extraordinary attraction.

History and Significance of the Dubai Frame :

The Dubai Frame was conceptualized as a part of the Dubai Municipality's initiative to create notable landmarks to enhance the city's skyline. Designed by award-winning architect Fernando Donis, the visionary behind Dubai's Porsche Design Towers, the Dubai Frame was envisioned as a monumental gateway connecting the city's rich heritage with its vibrant future. The project commenced in 2013 and was completed in 2017, marking a significant addition to Dubai's architectural landscape.

Architectural Design and Structure :

The Dubai Frame's design is a stunning fusion of modern aesthetics and cultural symbolism. The structure comprises two towering rectangular towers, each standing at a height of 150 meters, connected by a 93-meter bridge at the top. The exterior of the frame is adorned with a gold cladding, which imparts a majestic appearance to the structure.

Upon entering the Dubai Frame, visitors are transported to a multimedia exhibition that narrates the city's journey from its humble beginnings as a fishing village to its present status as a global metropolis. The exhibition showcases Dubai's impressive transformation through interactive displays, augmented reality, and visual presentations, immersing visitors in the city's rich history.

Dubai Frame's Sky Deck and Panoramic Views :

Ascending to the Sky Deck is the highlight of any visit to the Dubai Frame. Located at the topmost level of the structure, the observation deck offers panoramic views of Dubai's iconic landmarks and contrasting cityscapes. From one side of the deck, visitors can marvel at the historical districts of Dubai, such as Deira and Karama, with their traditional architecture and bustling markets. On the other side, the futuristic skyline of Downtown Dubai, featuring the Burj Khalifa and Dubai Mall, dominates the view.

The transparent glass floor of the Sky Deck adds a thrilling element, allowing visitors to experience a sensation of walking on air while gazing down at the city below. The panoramic elevators offer a mesmerizing ascent and descent, providing stunning views during the journey.

Interactive Exhibits and Virtual Reality :

Apart from the panoramic views, the Dubai Frame houses various interactive exhibits and immersive experiences that engage visitors of all ages. The virtual reality zone enables guests to explore Dubai's future projects and developments, offering a glimpse into the city's ambitious plans. The hologram tunnel presents captivating visual effects, creating a sense of wonder and intrigue.

Furthermore, the Dubai Frame features a 3D photo booth where visitors can capture unique moments against the backdrop of the city's iconic landmarks. The souvenir shop offers an array of Dubai-themed memorabilia, allowing visitors to take home a piece of the experience.

Practical Information for Visitors :

To ensure a smooth and enjoyable visit to the Dubai Frame, it is essential to have some practical information handy. The Dubai Frame is located in Zabeel Park, easily accessible by public transportation or private vehicles. The park also offers ample parking facilities for visitors. It is advisable to book tickets in advance to avoid long queues, especially during peak tourist seasons. The Dubai Frame is open from 9:00 AM to 9:00 PM, seven days a week.

Conclusion (approximately 200 words):

The Dubai Frame stands as an iconic symbol of Dubai's ambition, blending past and future in a captivating architectural masterpiece. Its remarkable design, panoramic views, and interactive exhibits make it a must-visit destination for travelers seeking a unique experience in Dubai. Whether you are a history enthusiast, an architecture lover, or simply someone looking to appreciate the beauty of Dubai, the Dubai Frame offers an unforgettable journey through time and space. As you step onto the Sky Deck and witness the mesmerizing vistas of old and new Dubai, you will truly understand why this architectural gem has become one of the city's most popular attractions.

CHAPTER EIGHT

Day Trips from Dubai

• *Abu Dhabi*

Dubai, a bustling metropolis known for its towering skyscrapers and lavish lifestyle, offers a myriad of attractions for tourists. While it has become a sought-after destination, neighboring Abu Dhabi often remains overlooked. However, just a short distance away from Dubai lies the capital city of the United Arab Emirates (UAE) - Abu Dhabi, which boasts its own unique charm and a wealth of cultural, historical, and modern attractions. In this Dubai travel guide, we will explore the wonders of Abu Dhabi and highlight why it deserves a place on your itinerary as an exciting day trip from Dubai.

Distance and Accessibility :

Abu Dhabi is located approximately 130 kilometers southwest of Dubai, making it an easily accessible destination for a day trip. Traveling between the two cities can be done conveniently by various modes of transportation. If you prefer a hassle-free journey, consider booking a guided tour that includes transportation from Dubai to Abu Dhabi, allowing you to sit back and enjoy the ride. Alternatively, public buses and taxis are available, offering flexibility for independent travelers. The journey takes around 1.5 to 2 hours, depending on traffic conditions.

Sheikh Zayed Grand Mosque :
A visit to Abu Dhabi would be incomplete without exploring the magnificent Sheikh Zayed Grand Mosque, one of the world's largest mosques. This architectural masterpiece is an awe-inspiring sight with its gleaming white marble and intricate Islamic designs. Visitors are welcome to admire the mosque's stunning features, including its grand prayer hall, reflecting pools, and over 80 marble domes. Respectful attire is required, and women must cover their heads.

Louvre Abu Dhabi :
Art enthusiasts will delight in a visit to the Louvre Abu Dhabi, a cultural landmark that houses an impressive collection of artworks from around the world. This collaboration between the UAE and France presents a fusion of Eastern and Western art in a stunning architectural setting. The museum's

galleries display an extensive range of artworks, from ancient artifacts to contemporary masterpieces. The Louvre Abu Dhabi offers a unique cultural experience that will enrich your understanding of art and history.

Yas Island :

For those seeking entertainment and thrill, Yas Island is a must-visit destination in Abu Dhabi. Located on a natural island, this entertainment hub is home to various attractions that cater to all ages. Motorsport enthusiasts can satisfy their need for speed at the iconic Yas Marina Circuit, which hosts the Formula 1 Abu Dhabi Grand Prix. Yas Waterworld, a sprawling water park, offers exciting water slides, wave pools, and lazy rivers. Additionally, Yas Island is renowned for its Ferrari-themed amusement park, Ferrari World Abu Dhabi, where visitors can experience exhilarating rides and learn about the iconic Italian brand.

Heritage Village :

To gain insight into Abu Dhabi's rich heritage, a visit to the Heritage Village is highly recommended. This reconstructed village provides a glimpse into the city's past, showcasing traditional Bedouin tents, ancient crafts, and local artifacts. Explore the traditional Emirati architecture, watch demonstrations of pottery and weaving, and indulge in authentic Emirati cuisine. The Heritage Village allows visitors to connect with Abu Dhabi's cultural roots and appreciate the local traditions.

Corniche and Beaches :
Abu Dhabi's Corniche is a picturesque waterfront promenade that stretches along the city's coastline, offering stunning views of the Arabian Gulf. Visitors can take leisurely strolls, rent bicycles, or simply relax on the pristine beaches. The Corniche is also home to various parks, playgrounds, and food stalls, providing a perfect setting for a family outing or a romantic evening walk. Enjoy the refreshing sea breeze and admire the city's skyline while immersing yourself in the serene ambiance.

Abu Dhabi, the capital city of the UAE, is an enticing destination that complements the vibrant atmosphere of Dubai. With its diverse range of attractions, including the awe-inspiring Sheikh Zayed Grand Mosque, the world-class Louvre Abu Dhabi, the thrill of Yas Island, the cultural experience at the Heritage Village, and the picturesque Corniche, Abu Dhabi promises an unforgettable day trip. Whether you are a history buff, an art lover, or an adventure seeker, this neighboring city is a perfect addition to your Dubai itinerary. Don't miss the opportunity to explore the wonders of Abu Dhabi while visiting Dubai.

•*Sharjah*

When it comes to exploring the United Arab Emirates (UAE), Dubai often steals the spotlight with its glitzy skyscrapers, luxurious shopping malls, and extravagant attractions. However, just a short distance away lies another gem that is often overlooked by tourists: Sharjah. Located just 25 kilometers northeast of Dubai, Sharjah is the third-largest emirate in the UAE and offers a rich cultural heritage, fascinating historical sites, and a vibrant art scene. In this Dubai travel guide, we will delve into the delights of Sharjah, showcasing why it deserves a spot on your itinerary as a day trip destination from Dubai.

I. The Cultural Capital of the UAE :
A. Historical Significance:

UNESCO World Heritage Sites: Sharjah boasts several UNESCO-listed sites, including the historic areas of Sharjah, Al Hisn, and the Arabian Peninsula's oldest souks.

Sharjah Fort (Al Hisn): Explore the beautifully restored fort that once served as the residence of the ruling family and played a significant role in the emirate's history.

Sharjah Museum of Islamic Civilization: Discover a vast collection of Islamic artifacts and art, showcasing the region's rich cultural heritage.

B. Art and Literature:

Sharjah Art Museum: Immerse yourself in the vibrant art scene of the UAE, featuring an impressive collection of contemporary and traditional artwork.

Sharjah Calligraphy Museum: Witness the intricate art of calligraphy and its historical significance in Islamic culture.

Sharjah International Book Fair: If your visit aligns with November, don't miss the largest book fair in the Arab world, attracting book lovers from around the globe.

II. Cultural Exploration :

A. Al Qasba: This waterfront development offers a range of attractions, including a Ferris wheel, a musical fountain, and a canal reminiscent of Venice.

B. Heritage Area:

Sharjah Heritage Museum: Gain insight into Emirati culture and traditions through interactive exhibits and displays.
Souq Al Arsah: Wander through the oldest souk in the UAE, known for its traditional handicrafts, spices, and unique shopping experience.
Sharjah Calligraphy Museum: Learn about the history and evolution of calligraphy, with exhibits showcasing various scripts and styles.

C. Central Market (Blue Souk): Indulge in a shopping spree at this iconic marketplace, known for its blue-tiled facade and a wide array of shops offering jewelry, textiles, and traditional Arabic handicrafts.

III. Natural Splendors :
A. Al Noor Island: Escape the city's hustle and bustle in this lush oasis, featuring beautifully landscaped gardens, art installations, and a butterfly house.
B. Al Majaz Waterfront: Relax by the waterfront promenade, enjoy stunning views of the Sharjah skyline, and catch dazzling water fountain shows in the evening.

C. Sharjah Aquarium and Maritime Museum: Delve into the world of marine life with captivating exhibits and interactive displays.

IV. *Family-Friendly Attractions:*

A. Sharjah Discovery Centre: A hands-on science museum designed for children, offering interactive exhibits and educational programs.

B. Al Montazah Parks: Enjoy a day of fun and excitement at this expansive park featuring water rides, play areas, and lush green spaces.

C. Sharjah Desert Park: Embark on a desert adventure within the city limits, where you can visit a wildlife center, botanical garden, and participate in camel rides.

While Dubai undoubtedly offers a plethora of attractions, a day trip to Sharjah presents an opportunity to delve deeper into the cultural roots and historical heritage of the UAE. With its UNESCO World Heritage Sites, thriving art scene, and family-friendly attractions, Sharjah offers a diverse range of experiences that will enrich your visit to the region. So, when planning your Dubai itinerary, make sure to set aside a day to explore the treasures of Sharjah and discover the hidden gems that lie just beyond Dubai's glittering skyline.

• *Al Ain*

Dubai, known for its glitz, glamour, and towering skyscrapers, offers a plethora of attractions and experiences. However, venturing beyond the city's bustling streets unveils a different side of the United Arab Emirates (UAE). Just a two-hour drive from Dubai lies Al Ain, a captivating oasis city that serves as a perfect day trip destination. This comprehensive Dubai travel guide explores the wonders of Al Ain, highlighting its rich history, cultural heritage, natural beauty, and attractions that make it an ideal excursion for visitors seeking a unique experience.

Historical and Cultural Significance
Al Ain is renowned for its deep-rooted historical and cultural heritage. As one of the oldest permanently inhabited settlements in the world, the city is home to numerous archaeological sites that provide insights into the region's ancient past. Al

Ain's UNESCO World Heritage Sites, such as the Hili Archaeological Park and the Jebel Hafeet Tombs, offer a glimpse into the city's prehistoric civilizations.

Additionally, Al Ain boasts several captivating museums, including the Al Ain National Museum and the Al Ain Palace Museum, which provide a deeper understanding of the UAE's traditions and customs. Visitors can immerse themselves in the local culture by exploring the exhibits showcasing artifacts, traditional crafts, and historical artifacts.

Natural Beauty and Outdoor Activities

Al Ain's picturesque landscapes and natural wonders make it a paradise for nature enthusiasts. The city is surrounded by the majestic Jebel Hafeet mountain range, offering breathtaking views and fantastic hiking opportunities. Climbing to the summit rewards visitors with panoramic vistas of the cityscape and the vast desert beyond.

The city is also blessed with numerous green spaces and parks, including the Al Ain Oasis, a UNESCO World Heritage Site. This expansive oasis boasts thousands of date palms and traditional aflaj irrigation systems, providing a tranquil environment for leisurely strolls or picnics. Exploring the oasis on foot or by bicycle allows visitors to appreciate the serene beauty and learn about traditional farming practices.

Family-Friendly Attractions

Al Ain caters to families seeking fun-filled activities and educational experiences. The Al Ain Zoo, one of the largest in the Middle East, offers an opportunity to get up close to a diverse range of animal species, including endangered species and exotic birds. The zoo's conservation efforts and interactive exhibits provide an educational and entertaining experience for visitors of all ages.

For adventure seekers, Al Ain's Wadi Adventure is a thrilling destination. This water park offers a variety of water-based activities, such as white-water rafting, kayaking, and surfing, providing an adrenaline-pumping escape from the desert heat.

Shopping and Dining

Al Ain offers a unique shopping experience that combines traditional souks with modern retail outlets. The bustling Al Ain Souk is a treasure trove of spices, textiles, handicrafts, and traditional Emirati products, allowing visitors to immerse themselves in the local market culture. Additionally, Al Ain boasts several shopping malls, including the Al Ain Mall and Bawadi Mall, offering a range of international brands and entertainment options.

Culinary enthusiasts will find a diverse range of dining options in Al Ain, from authentic Emirati cuisine to international flavors. Traditional Arabic restaurants, such as Al Fanar and Al Ain Palace Restaurant, serve delicious local dishes in an authentic setting.

Al Ain, with its rich historical significance, natural beauty, family-friendly attractions, and shopping delights, is an excellent day trip option for visitors to Dubai. Exploring Al Ain allows travelers to delve into the UAE's heritage and experience a more traditional side of the country, away from the glitz and glamour of Dubai. Whether it's immersing oneself in history, marveling at natural landscapes, embarking on thrilling adventures, or indulging in local cuisine, Al Ain offers a well-rounded experience that complements the cosmopolitan allure of Dubai. So, when planning your trip to Dubai, be sure to set aside a day to discover the wonders of Al Ain and create unforgettable memories.

• *Fujairah*

Fujairah, a neighboring emirate located on the eastern coast of the United Arab Emirates (UAE), presents an ideal day trip destination for those seeking a change of scenery. This Dubai travel guide will delve into the wonders of Fujairah, highlighting its natural beauty, cultural heritage, and intriguing historical sites that make it an excellent choice for an unforgettable day trip from Dubai.

I. Getting to Fujairah

Before embarking on a day trip to Fujairah, it's essential to plan the journey. The most convenient way to reach Fujairah from Dubai is by road. The approximate driving time is around 90 minutes, with well-maintained highways ensuring a smooth journey. Renting a car or hiring a private driver offers flexibility and convenience. Alternatively, organized tours and shuttle services are available for those who prefer not to drive.

II. Natural Splendors

Fujairah boasts a diverse range of natural attractions, making it a haven for outdoor enthusiasts. Here are some must-visit sites:

Fujairah Beaches: The emirate is home to pristine beaches with turquoise waters and soft white sands. Al Aqah Beach and Sandy Beach Park are popular choices, offering relaxation and water activities like snorkeling, jet skiing, and paddleboarding.

Hajar Mountains: Fujairah is nestled against the Hajar Mountains, creating a stunning backdrop for the region. Nature lovers can explore the rugged terrain, hike scenic trails, and revel in breathtaking panoramic views.

Wadi Adventures: For adrenaline junkies, Wadi Adventures is a must-visit destination. Located near the Hajar Mountains, this adventure park offers thrilling activities such as white water rafting, kayaking, zip-lining, and rock climbing.

III. Cultural Heritage
Fujairah has a rich cultural heritage, and exploring its historical and cultural sites provides a deeper understanding of the region. Here are a few noteworthy attractions:

Fujairah Fort: This ancient fort, built in the 17th century, is one of Fujairah's most iconic landmarks. Visitors can explore its restored interiors, including a museum that showcases traditional Emirati life and artifacts.

Al Bidyah Mosque: Known as the oldest mosque in the UAE, Al Bidyah Mosque dates back to the 15th century. Its unique architecture, with its mud-brick walls and four domes, is a testament to the region's Islamic heritage.

Fujairah Museum: History buffs can delve into Fujairah's past at the Fujairah Museum, which exhibits archaeological artifacts, traditional costumes, and weaponry, offering insights into the emirate's history and culture.

IV. Aquatic Adventures

Fujairah's pristine coastline and rich marine life make it an exceptional destination for water-based activities:

Snorkeling and Diving: Fujairah's clear waters are teeming with vibrant coral reefs and diverse marine species. Snorkeling and diving enthusiasts can explore underwater worlds and discover the beauty of the Arabian Gulf.

Snoopy Island: Situated off the coast of Fujairah, Snoopy Island is a renowned snorkeling and diving spot. Named after its resemblance to the famous Peanuts character, the island's crystal-clear waters and colorful marine life create a memorable experience.

Boat Tours: Embarking on a boat tour around Fujairah allows visitors to witness the emirate's coastline from a different perspective. These tours often include opportunities for swimming, fishing, and even dolphin watching.

V. Culinary Delights
Exploring Fujairah is incomplete without savoring its culinary offerings. Traditional Emirati cuisine and international flavors await visitors in various establishments:

Local Delicacies: Sample Emirati dishes such as machbous (spiced rice with meat), harees (slow-cooked wheat and meat), and luqaimat (sweet dumplings). Al Meshwar Restaurant in Fujairah City is highly recommended for authentic Emirati cuisine.

Seafood Extravaganza: Being a coastal emirate, Fujairah excels in fresh seafood. Seafood restaurants along the coast offer delectable dishes, from grilled prawns and lobster to fish curries and biryanis.

International Cuisine: Fujairah's dining scene caters to various tastes, with international restaurants serving Indian, Chinese, Italian, and other global cuisines. From fine dining establishments to casual eateries, there's something for everyone.

Fujairah, just a short drive away from Dubai, offers a captivating blend of natural beauty, cultural heritage, and exciting activities that make it an excellent choice for a day trip. From its pristine beaches and majestic mountains to its historic forts and underwater wonders, Fujairah provides a refreshing change of pace from the cosmopolitan charm of Dubai. Whether seeking relaxation, adventure, or a deeper understanding of Emirati culture, Fujairah has it all. So, when planning your next Dubai itinerary, consider adding a day trip to Fujairah for an unforgettable experience that will leave you with cherished memories of the UAE's captivating diversity.

- **Hatta**

Located in the picturesque Hajar Mountains, Hatta is a hidden gem nestled in the heart of Dubai's desert landscape. Renowned for its natural beauty, cultural heritage, and outdoor adventures, Hatta offers a refreshing escape from the bustling city life of Dubai. This article serves as a comprehensive guide for travelers looking to embark on a memorable day trip to Hatta from Dubai.

History and Cultural Significance
Hatta boasts a rich historical and cultural heritage that dates back centuries. Originally settled by the Hajarain tribe, the town was an important trading hub due to its strategic location between the Arabian Gulf and Oman. Throughout its history, Hatta has been influenced by various civilizations, including the Portuguese and the British.

Travelers can explore the Hatta Heritage Village, which provides a glimpse into the traditional Emirati way of life. The village showcases restored houses, a fort, and a museum that displays artifacts and exhibits depicting the region's history. Visitors can also witness traditional handicrafts, such as pottery and weaving, being practiced by local artisans.

Natural Attractions

Hatta is renowned for its stunning natural beauty, offering a myriad of outdoor activities for nature enthusiasts. The Hatta Dam, a picturesque reservoir surrounded by rugged mountains, is a must-visit destination. Visitors can enjoy various water-based activities like kayaking, paddleboarding, and fishing in the tranquil waters of the dam.

For those seeking adventure, the Hatta Mountain Bike Trail Centre offers thrilling biking trails suitable for all skill levels. With its diverse terrains and breathtaking vistas, this trail center is a haven for mountain bikers. Hiking enthusiasts can explore the rugged trails of the Hatta Mountains, which offer panoramic views and an opportunity to witness the region's unique flora and fauna.

Another notable attraction is the Hatta Rock Pools, a series of natural pools formed by the Wadi Hatta. Surrounded by rocky landscapes and lush vegetation, these pools offer a refreshing oasis for visitors to swim and relax in a natural setting.

Heritage Sites and Architecture

Hatta is home to several architectural gems that showcase the region's heritage. The Hatta Fort, dating back to the 16th century, stands as a testament to the town's historical significance. Visitors can explore the fort's interior and learn about its role in protecting the town from invasions.

The Juma Mosque, constructed in traditional Arabian style, is another notable landmark in Hatta. With its striking white facade and intricate calligraphy, the mosque provides a serene ambiance for prayer and reflection.

Excursions and Activities

Apart from its natural and cultural attractions, Hatta offers various excursions and activities to engage visitors. One of the highlights is the Hatta Kayak, a unique experience where travelers can paddle through the calm waters of the Hatta Dam, surrounded by the rugged mountains.

For those seeking adrenaline-pumping adventures, Hatta Zipline allows participants to soar above the breathtaking Hajar Mountains, providing a thrilling bird's-eye view of the region's natural beauty.

Hatta Wadi Hub is another popular destination that caters to adventure seekers. Activities such as dune bashing, off-road driving, archery, and axe throwing are available, ensuring an action-packed day for visitors.

Dining and Accommodation

Hatta offers a range of dining options that showcase traditional Emirati cuisine alongside international flavors. Local restaurants serve delicacies like Mandi (slow-cooked meat and rice) and Majboos (spiced meat and rice), providing a tantalizing culinary experience for visitors.

While Hatta is primarily a day trip destination, there are a few accommodations available for those who wish to extend their stay. Hatta Sedr Trailers Resort provides unique lodging in retro-style trailers, allowing guests to immerse themselves in the natural surroundings. Hatta Damani Lodges and Hatta Caravan Park are other options offering comfortable accommodations amidst the scenic beauty of Hatta.

Hatta, with its historical significance, natural wonders, and exciting activities, is a perfect day trip destination from Dubai. Whether you're interested in immersing yourself in cultural heritage, indulging in outdoor adventures, or simply enjoying the tranquility of nature, Hatta has something for everyone. A visit to Hatta promises an enriching experience that showcases the beauty and diversity of the United Arab Emirates. So, if you're planning a trip to Dubai, don't miss the opportunity to embark on an unforgettable day trip to Hatta and create memories that will last a lifetime.

CHAPTER NINE

Outdoor Adventures

• *Dubai Desert Conservation Reserve*

Dubai, a vibrant and modern city known for its towering skyscrapers and luxurious lifestyle, may seem like an unlikely place to find a nature reserve. However, nestled amidst the city's glitz and glamour lies the Dubai Desert Conservation Reserve (DDCR), a remarkable testament to the Emirate's commitment to environmental conservation. Spanning over 225 square kilometers, this protected area serves as a sanctuary for native wildlife, a hub for sustainable tourism, and an educational platform for raising awareness about desert ecosystems. In this comprehensive Dubai travel guide, we delve into the unique features of the Dubai Desert Conservation Reserve and why it is a must-visit destination for nature enthusiasts and adventure seekers alike.

History and Creation of the Dubai Desert Conservation Reserve:
The Dubai Desert Conservation Reserve was established in 2003 under the visionary guidance of His Highness Sheikh Mohammed bin Rashid Al Maktoum, the ruler of Dubai. Recognizing the importance of preserving the Emirate's natural heritage, he designated a vast expanse of desert as a protected area. This pioneering initiative aimed to safeguard the fragile desert ecosystem and promote sustainable tourism practices.

Biodiversity and Wildlife:
Despite the arid conditions, the Dubai Desert Conservation Reserve is home to a surprising array of flora and fauna. The reserve boasts a diverse range of native wildlife, including the Arabian oryx, gazelles, sand gazelles, desert foxes, and numerous bird species. These remarkable creatures have adapted to the harsh desert environment, and observing them in their natural habitat is a unique experience that allows visitors to appreciate their resilience and beauty.

Conservation Efforts:
The primary objective of the Dubai Desert Conservation Reserve is to protect the delicate desert ecosystem and restore its natural balance.

The reserve implements several conservation initiatives, including habitat restoration, reforestation programs, and the reintroduction of endangered species. These efforts have proven successful, as evidenced by the steady increase in the Arabian oryx population, which was once on the brink of extinction.

Sustainable Tourism and Experiential Activities:

The Dubai Desert Conservation Reserve offers a range of sustainable tourism activities that allow visitors to immerse themselves in the desert environment while minimizing their impact on nature. Guided nature walks, wildlife drives, and camel treks provide unique opportunities to explore the reserve's diverse landscapes and encounter its resident wildlife. Additionally, the reserve offers a captivating stargazing experience, allowing visitors to marvel at the desert sky's celestial wonders.

Conservation Education and Research:

The DDCR plays a crucial role in raising awareness about desert conservation and sustainable practices. The reserve hosts educational programs, workshops, and interactive exhibits to engage visitors of all ages. These initiatives highlight the importance of preserving the desert ecosystem and emphasize the role individuals can play in environmental conservation. The DDCR also collaborates with research institutions to conduct scientific studies, contributing valuable insights into desert ecology and promoting conservation-oriented decision-making.

Infrastructure and Facilities:
To enhance visitors' experiences, the Dubai Desert Conservation Reserve offers well-designed infrastructure and facilities. The Al Maha Desert Resort and Spa, an eco-friendly luxury resort within the reserve, provides a serene and immersive desert experience. The resort blends seamlessly with the surrounding environment and offers stunning views of the reserve. Furthermore, visitors can enjoy dining experiences that showcase traditional Arabian cuisine and culture.

Conservation Beyond Boundaries:
The success of the Dubai Desert Conservation Reserve has inspired similar conservation initiatives within the UAE and globally. The model of combining environmental preservation with sustainable tourism has gained recognition as a viable approach to protect fragile ecosystems while promoting economic growth. The Dubai government's commitment to sustainability extends

beyond the DDCR, with the Emirate implementing various eco-friendly policies and initiatives citywide.

The Dubai Desert Conservation Reserve stands as a testament to Dubai's dedication to environmental conservation and sustainable tourism. Amidst the city's modernity and fast-paced development, the reserve offers a serene and captivating experience, allowing visitors to reconnect with nature and appreciate the beauty of the desert ecosystem. Through its conservation efforts, educational initiatives, and sustainable tourism practices, the DDCR sets an example for the world, showcasing the harmonious coexistence of a thriving city and a preserved natural environment. A visit to the Dubai Desert Conservation Reserve is not only an opportunity to explore the wonders of the desert but also a chance to contribute to the ongoing preservation of our planet's precious ecosystems.

•*Diving and Snorkeling*

Dubai, known for its awe-inspiring skyscrapers and luxurious lifestyle, also offers a fascinating world beneath its azure waters. The Emirate's coastal location on the Arabian Gulf makes it a perfect destination for diving and snorkeling enthusiasts. With vibrant coral reefs, abundant marine life, and excellent visibility, Dubai's underwater realm promises unforgettable experiences. In this comprehensive Dubai travel guide, we will delve into the captivating world of diving and snorkeling, exploring the top dive sites, diving operators, safety guidelines, and additional tips to make the most of your underwater adventures.

I. Dive Sites in Dubai

Dubai boasts a diverse array of dive sites that cater to both novice and experienced divers. Here are some of the top dive sites worth exploring:

The World Islands: This iconic archipelago of man-made islands offers unique diving opportunities. Each island represents a different country, and the submerged structures attract a myriad of marine life, including rays, turtles, and colorful reef fish.

Dubai Aquarium & Underwater Zoo: Located within the Dubai Mall, this indoor dive site provides an extraordinary experience. Certified divers can explore the vast aquarium and encounter over 30,000 marine creatures, including sharks, stingrays, and schools of tropical fish.

Martini Rock: Situated off the coast of Jebel Ali, Martini Rock offers an excellent dive for experienced divers. The submerged rock formation is home to a variety of marine species, such as barracudas, angelfish, and moray eels. The site features vibrant coral gardens and an exciting swim-through cave.

Dibba Rock: Located near the UAE's border with Oman, Dibba Rock is a popular dive spot accessible from Dubai. This site boasts stunning coral formations, including brain, mushroom, and table corals. Divers can encounter turtles, reef sharks, and an abundance of colorful reef fish.

II. Snorkeling Hotspots
For those who prefer snorkeling, Dubai offers several captivating locations to explore the underwater world at a more leisurely pace. Here are some top snorkeling hotspots:

Jumeirah Beach: Located along Dubai's coastline, Jumeirah Beach offers easy access to clear and calm waters, making it an ideal spot for snorkeling. Snorkelers can discover vibrant coral gardens, encounter tropical fish, and even spot rays and turtles.

Snoopy Island: Situated in Fujairah, just a short drive from Dubai, Snoopy Island is a snorkeler's paradise. This small island is surrounded by crystal-clear waters teeming with marine life, including parrotfish, clownfish, and pufferfish. Snorkelers can explore the colorful corals and revel in the tranquility of the area.

Zabeel Saray Lagoon: Located near Palm Jumeirah, the Zabeel Saray Lagoon offers a unique snorkeling experience. The lagoon is home to an artificial reef, which serves as a sanctuary for various marine species. Snorkelers can witness the transformation of this man-made ecosystem and observe its thriving biodiversity.

III. Diving and Snorkeling Operators
Dubai boasts a range of diving and snorkeling operators that provide guided tours and equipment rentals. Some renowned operators include:

Al Boom Diving: With multiple branches in Dubai, Al Boom Diving offers a wide range of diving courses for beginners and advanced divers. They also organize diving trips to popular dive sites, providing a safe and enjoyable experience.

Divers Down: Known for their professional and friendly staff, Divers Down offers diving and snorkeling excursions in Dubai. They cater to all levels of experience and ensure personalized attention to divers and snorkelers.

Nemo Diving Center: Located in Jumeirah Beach Hotel, Nemo Diving Center offers diving and snorkeling activities for all ages and skill levels. Their certified instructors provide comprehensive training and guide participants to some of Dubai's best underwater spots.

IV. Safety Guidelines and Tips
To ensure a safe and enjoyable diving or snorkeling experience, it is essential to adhere to the following guidelines:

Choose a reputable operator: Opt for licensed diving and snorkeling operators with experienced instructors and well-maintained equipment.

Check weather conditions: Before heading out, check weather forecasts and sea conditions. Avoid diving or snorkeling during rough seas or inclement weather.

Dive within your limits: If you are a beginner or have limited diving experience, stick to dive sites suitable for your skill level. Do not push yourself beyond your capabilities.

Practice responsible diving: Respect marine life and coral reefs by avoiding touching or damaging them. Do not feed or harass marine creatures, as this can disrupt their natural behavior.

Dubai's underwater world offers a mesmerizing escape from the bustling cityscape, allowing visitors to explore vibrant coral reefs and encounter a myriad of marine species. Whether you choose to dive deep in7to the Arabian Gulf or snorkel along the pristine beaches, Dubai provides a plethora of opportunities for underwater enthusiasts. By following safety guidelines, choosing reputable operators, and respecting the marine environment, you can embark on a remarkable diving and snorkeling adventure in Dubai, creating memories that will last a lifetime.

•*Skydiving*

Among the myriad of activities available, skydiving stands out as a heart-pounding experience that offers an unparalleled adrenaline rush. With its stunning skyline, breathtaking landscapes, and perfect weather conditions, Dubai has become a global hub for skydiving enthusiasts. In this comprehensive Dubai travel guide, we will delve into the world of skydiving in Dubai, exploring the exhilarating jumps, safety measures, and the top skydiving locations that make Dubai an unrivaled destination for adventure seekers.

Skydiving in Dubai: An Overview

Skydiving is the ultimate adventure sport that allows individuals to experience the thrill of freefalling from thousands of feet above the ground, followed by a peaceful descent while enjoying the awe-inspiring views. The popularity of skydiving in

Dubai has skyrocketed in recent years, attracting both beginners and experienced skydivers from around the globe.

Safety Precautions and Training

Prioritizing safety is paramount in skydiving, and Dubai maintains rigorous safety standards to ensure a secure and enjoyable experience for all participants. Before embarking on a skydiving adventure, participants must undergo comprehensive training sessions conducted by certified instructors. These sessions cover essential topics such as equipment usage, body positioning, emergency procedures, and parachute deployment. Dubai's skydiving centers adhere to strict protocols and maintain state-of-the-art equipment to maximize safety.

Tandem Skydiving: The Perfect Introduction
For first-time skydivers, tandem skydiving is the ideal option. In tandem skydiving, participants are securely harnessed to an experienced instructor, who takes care of all technical aspects during the jump. This allows beginners to savor the thrill of skydiving without the need for extensive training or prior experience. Tandem jumps provide an opportunity to witness Dubai's awe-inspiring landscapes, including the Palm Jumeirah, Burj

Khalifa, and the Arabian Desert, from a unique perspective.

Accelerated Freefall (AFF): The Path to Independence

For those seeking a more immersive skydiving experience, Dubai offers Accelerated Freefall (AFF) courses. This training program enables participants to progress from tandem jumps to solo skydiving, ultimately leading to obtaining a skydiving license. The AFF course involves rigorous training modules that focus on essential skills, including stable body positioning, altitude awareness, and controlled canopy deployment. Dubai's skydiving centers provide AFF courses conducted by highly skilled instructors, ensuring participants develop the necessary skills and confidence to dive solo.

Skydiving Locations in Dubai

Dubai boasts a selection of top-notch skydiving locations that provide breathtaking vistas and exhilarating jumps. The most renowned skydiving center in Dubai is Skydive Dubai, located in the picturesque Palm Jumeirah. Here, skydivers can experience the thrill of a tandem jump while gazing at the iconic Palm Jumeirah archipelago and the azure waters of the Arabian Gulf. Another popular location is the Desert Campus Dropzone, situated amidst the captivating beauty of the Arabian Desert. The Desert Campus offers a unique skydiving experience, combining the adrenaline rush of the jump with awe-inspiring desert views.

Choosing the Right Time to Skydive
Dubai's climate plays a crucial role in determining the best time to indulge in skydiving. The winter months, from November to March, offer the most favorable weather conditions, with clear skies, mild temperatures, and low humidity. During this period, the scorching heat of Dubai's summer is replaced by more pleasant temperatures, ensuring a comfortable and enjoyable skydiving experience.

Tips for an Unforgettable Skydiving Experience
To make the most of your skydiving adventure in Dubai, consider the following tips:

a. Dress comfortably: Wear appropriate clothing that allows freedom of movement and protects against wind chill.
b. Arrive early: Reach the skydiving center ahead of time to complete the necessary paperwork and training sessions without rushing.
c. Capture the memories: Many skydiving centers offer photo and video packages to document your

exhilarating experience. Consider availing these services to relive the thrill and share your adventure with others.

d. Embrace the fear: Skydiving can be an intimidating experience, but embracing the fear and stepping out of your comfort zone will reward you with an unforgettable adventure.

Skydiving in Dubai offers an unmatched adventure, allowing thrill-seekers to experience an adrenaline rush like no other. With world-class facilities, highly trained instructors, and stunning aerial views, Dubai has solidified its reputation as a premier skydiving destination. Whether you choose a tandem jump or embark on the path to becoming a licensed skydiver, Dubai promises an unforgettable experience that will leave you with lifelong memories. So, gear up, take the leap, and immerse yourself in the awe-inspiring world of skydiving in Dubai!

• *Hot Air Ballooning*

Dubai, a mesmerizing city known for its modern architecture, luxurious resorts, and vibrant culture, offers visitors a unique opportunity to embark on a thrilling hot air ballooning adventure. Floating above the vast Arabian Desert and witnessing the breathtaking sunrise or sunset vistas is an experience like no other. This comprehensive Dubai travel guide unveils the magic of hot air ballooning, providing essential information on the experience, safety measures, and the best hot air ballooning operators in Dubai.

The Hot Air Ballooning Experience
Hot air ballooning in Dubai is an exhilarating activity that allows adventurers to soar above the city's iconic skyline and embrace the serenity of the desert. The experience typically starts before dawn, with participants gathering at the launch site. As the balloons are inflated and prepared for flight, anticipation builds, and soon passengers are gently lifted off the ground.

Once airborne, travelers are treated to awe-inspiring panoramic views of Dubai's stunning landscapes. The radiant sun casting its warm hues on the golden dunes below, the distant city skyline with its towering skyscrapers, and the tranquility of the desert create an unforgettable sight. The gentle breeze carries the balloon along, providing a peaceful and serene atmosphere, interrupted only by the occasional roar of the burners that keep the balloon aloft.

Safety Measures and Precautions

Hot air ballooning operators in Dubai prioritize the safety of their passengers. Before embarking on the adventure, participants are provided with detailed safety instructions. It is essential to follow these guidelines to ensure a secure and enjoyable experience. Some common safety measures include:

a. Pre-flight Briefing: Passengers receive a comprehensive pre-flight briefing that covers safety protocols, landing procedures, and emergency protocols. This information equips participants with the knowledge needed to have a safe journey.

b. Experienced Pilots: Dubai boasts a skilled team of experienced hot air balloon pilots who possess extensive knowledge of the local weather conditions and flight patterns. These professionals undergo rigorous training and are well-versed in all safety protocols.

c. Regular Maintenance and Inspections: The hot air balloons used in Dubai are regularly inspected and maintained to ensure their airworthiness and safety. These inspections include checking the burner systems, envelope fabric, basket integrity, and other essential components.

d. Weather Monitoring: Weather conditions play a crucial role in the safety of hot air ballooning. Operators closely monitor weather forecasts and conditions before each flight to ensure safe flying conditions. If unfavorable weather is detected, flights may be rescheduled or canceled for the safety of passengers.

Best Hot Air Ballooning Operators in Dubai
Dubai is home to several reputable hot air ballooning operators, each offering unique experiences and exceptional service. Here are some of the top operators to consider:

a. Balloon Adventures Emirates: With over a decade of experience, Balloon Adventures Emirates is one of the leading hot air balloon operators in Dubai. They offer unforgettable flights over the pristine desert landscape, complete with a gourmet breakfast and falconry demonstration upon landing.

b. Platinum Heritage: Platinum Heritage provides a premium hot air ballooning experience, combining desert wildlife encounters and cultural experiences with the balloon flight. Passengers can witness the native flora and fauna of the desert while enjoying a traditional Arabian breakfast.

c. Balloon Adventures Dubai: This operator offers a variety of flight options, including shared and private experiences. With their state-of-the-art balloons and highly skilled pilots, Balloon Adventures Dubai promises a safe and exhilarating journey through the Dubai skies.

d. Skydive Dubai Balloon: Known for their professionalism and safety standards, Skydive Dubai Balloon offers a thrilling hot air balloon adventure with stunning views of the Dubai Desert Conservation Reserve. The experience also includes a delicious breakfast in a traditional desert setting.

Tips for a Memorable Hot Air Ballooning Experience

To make the most of your hot air ballooning adventure in Dubai, consider the following tips:

a. Dress Comfortably: Wear comfortable clothing and closed-toe shoes suitable for outdoor activities. Layers are recommended, as temperatures can vary during the early morning flights.

b. Bring a Camera: Capture the breathtaking views and unforgettable moments during your hot air balloon ride. A camera or smartphone with sufficient battery and storage is essential.

c. Be Punctual: Arrive at the meeting point on time to ensure a smooth departure. Balloons typically take off early in the morning to catch the mesmerizing sunrise, so plan accordingly.

d. Stay Hydrated: Drink plenty of water before and after the flight to stay hydrated. Although the weather may be cool during the flight, it's important to remain hydrated in the desert environment.

Hot air ballooning in Dubai offers a unique perspective of the city and its mesmerizing surroundings. Soaring above the desert, passengers can witness Dubai's contrasting landscapes, from the vast dunes to the iconic skyline. With reputable operators prioritizing safety, adventurers can embark on this exhilarating journey with peace of mind.

As you plan your visit to Dubai, make sure to include hot air ballooning on your itinerary for an unforgettable experience. Remember to choose a reputable operator, follow safety guidelines, and prepare accordingly for the adventure. Whether you opt for a shared or private flight, hot air ballooning in Dubai promises breathtaking views and cherished memories that will last a lifetime. So, get ready to embark on an extraordinary journey and let your spirits soar high above the Arabian Desert.

•*Water Sports*

Dubai, the crown jewel of the United Arab Emirates, is renowned for its luxurious lifestyle, architectural marvels, and vibrant cosmopolitan ambiance. However, beyond its gleaming skyscrapers and desert landscapes, Dubai offers a breathtaking array of water sports that cater to thrill-seekers and water enthusiasts from around the world. From adrenaline-pumping jet skiing to tranquil paddleboarding, the emirate presents a diverse range of water activities to suit all preferences and skill levels. In this comprehensive Dubai travel guide, we will delve into the captivating world of water sports in Dubai, highlighting popular activities, top locations, safety measures, and everything you need to know to make the most of your aquatic adventure.

I. Thrilling Water Sports in Dubai :

Jet Skiing: Dubai's warm waters provide the perfect setting for jet skiing, a high-speed aquatic escapade. Visitors can rent jet skis from various locations along the coastline, including Jumeirah Beach and Dubai Marina. Expert instructors are available for beginners, ensuring a safe and exhilarating experience as you zoom across the azure waters of the Arabian Gulf.

Flyboarding: For those seeking an extraordinary experience, flyboarding combines elements of jetpacking and water sports. Equipped with a jet-propelled board, adventurers can soar above the water's surface, propelled by powerful water jets. Locations such as The Palm Jumeirah and JBR Beach offer flyboarding opportunities with professional trainers to guide participants.

Parasailing: Take to the skies and savor panoramic views of Dubai's iconic landmarks as you parasail over the glittering coastline. Dubai's professional parasailing operators guarantee a safe and unforgettable adventure, allowing you to enjoy breathtaking vistas of the city's skyline and pristine beaches.

Wakeboarding: Wakeboarding enthusiasts can indulge in the emirate's world-class wakeboarding facilities, such as the Dubai Marina Yacht Club. With its calm waters and state-of-the-art equipment, Dubai provides an ideal environment for both beginners and advanced riders to showcase their skills and enjoy this thrilling water sport.

II. Serene Water Sports in Dubai :

Stand-up Paddleboarding (SUP): SUP has gained popularity in Dubai due to its tranquil nature and accessibility. Beginners can easily learn to balance and paddle on calm waters, while more experienced paddlers can explore the city's captivating waterways, such as the Dubai Canal or the Palm Jumeirah. SUP yoga classes are also available for those seeking a unique wellness experience.

Kayaking: Embark on a peaceful kayaking adventure and explore Dubai's hidden gems, including mangroves, lagoons, and winding creeks. Kayak rentals are available at various locations, providing an opportunity to witness the emirate's diverse marine and birdlife up close.

Snorkeling and Scuba Diving: Dubai's warm waters are teeming with vibrant marine life, making it an excellent destination for underwater exploration. Snorkeling and scuba diving enthusiasts can dive into an underwater wonderland filled with colorful coral reefs, tropical fish, and even shipwrecks. Dive centers across Dubai offer diving courses, guided tours, and equipment rentals for both beginners and experienced divers.

Sailing: Discover the beauty of Dubai's coastline aboard a luxury yacht or a traditional Arabian dhow. Enjoy a leisurely cruise along the tranquil waters, marvel at the iconic skyline, and relish a sumptuous dinner while basking in the gentle sea breeze. Numerous operators offer sailing experiences, ranging from romantic sunset cruises to private charters for larger groups.

III. Safety Measures and Considerations :

Qualified Instructors and Operators: When participating in water sports, it is essential to choose reputable operators that prioritize safety. Ensure that instructors are certified and experienced, and that they provide proper safety equipment and guidelines.

Weather Conditions: Stay informed about the weather forecast before engaging in water activities. Avoid venturing out during rough sea conditions or inclement weather, as it may pose unnecessary risks.

Swimming Ability: While some water sports require advanced swimming skills, others are suitable for beginners. Assess your swimming ability and choose activities accordingly. It is advisable to wear life jackets or personal flotation devices, especially for activities in deeper waters.

Sun Protection: Dubai's sun can be intense, even during cooler months. Apply sunscreen generously, wear protective clothing, and stay hydrated to avoid sunburn and dehydration.

Respect for Marine Environment: Practice responsible tourism by respecting the marine environment. Avoid littering, touching or damaging corals, and adhere to guidelines provided by instructors to preserve the delicate ecosystem.

Dubai's water sports scene offers an unparalleled opportunity to explore the emirate's stunning coastline and indulge in thrilling or tranquil aquatic adventures. Whether you seek an adrenaline rush or a serene connection with nature, Dubai's diverse range of water sports has something for everyone.

From jet skiing and parasailing to paddleboarding and snorkeling, visitors can embrace the emirate's stunning marine environment and create memories that will last a lifetime. However, it is crucial to prioritize safety, follow guidelines provided by certified instructors, and respect the marine ecosystem. So, prepare to embark on a mesmerizing aquatic journey in Dubai and discover the perfect blend of excitement, relaxation, and natural beauty that awaits you in this remarkable city.

•*Dubai Parks and Resorts*

Dubai, the dazzling city known for its grandeur and luxury, offers an unparalleled array of attractions and entertainment options for visitors from around the world. One of the prominent destinations that epitomizes Dubai's commitment to creating larger-than-life experiences is Dubai Parks and

Resorts. This expansive leisure and entertainment complex is a must-visit for anyone seeking thrilling adventures, family-friendly fun, and unforgettable memories. In this comprehensive travel guide, we will explore the various theme parks, attractions, accommodations, dining options, and practical information that will help you plan your visit to Dubai Parks and Resorts.

Location and Accessibility:

Dubai Parks and Resorts is situated in Jebel Ali, along Sheikh Zayed Road, making it easily accessible from both Dubai and Abu Dhabi. The complex is conveniently located approximately a 45-minute drive from Dubai International Airport, ensuring smooth and hassle-free transportation for visitors arriving by air. Moreover, there are numerous taxi services, private shuttles, and public transportation options available, making it effortless to reach the destination from any part of the city.

Theme Parks and Attractions:

Dubai Parks and Resorts is home to three major theme parks, a water park, and a family entertainment center, providing a wide range of experiences to suit every age group and interest.

Motiongate Dubai: This Hollywood-inspired theme park is a cinematic wonderland, featuring thrilling rides, live shows, and attractions based on popular movie franchises like Shrek, The Hunger Games, and Ghostbusters. From heart-pounding roller coasters to immersive 4D experiences, Motiongate Dubai offers an adrenaline-filled adventure for movie enthusiasts.

Bollywood Parks Dubai: Step into the magical world of Indian cinema at Bollywood Parks Dubai. Celebrating the vibrant culture of Bollywood, this park offers captivating live performances, dazzling musicals, and interactive attractions inspired by iconic Indian movies. Visitors can enjoy colorful street performances, behind-the-scenes tours, and delicious Indian cuisine while immersing themselves in the glitz and glamour of Bollywood.

Legoland Dubai: Perfect for families with young children, Legoland Dubai is a wonderland of creativity and imagination. The park features numerous Lego-themed rides, interactive attractions, and building experiences where kids can construct their own Lego masterpieces. From driving a Lego car to exploring a Lego city, Legoland Dubai promises a day filled with fun, education, and excitement for the entire family.

Legoland Water Park: Adjacent to Legoland Dubai, the Legoland Water Park is a refreshing oasis offering a splashing good time. With a variety of water slides, wave pools, and interactive play areas, this water park provides endless aquatic adventures for all ages. It's the perfect place to cool off and have a blast on a sunny Dubai day.

Riverland Dubai: Acting as the gateway to Dubai Parks and Resorts, Riverland Dubai is a vibrant themed district that brings together dining, shopping, and entertainment. Divided into four themed zones—The French Village, Boardwalk, India Gate, and The Peninsula—Riverland Dubai offers a unique blend of architectural styles, live performances, and a wide array of international cuisine, ensuring visitors have an enjoyable time before or after their park experiences.

Accommodations:
To enhance the overall experience, Dubai Parks and Resorts offers a range of on-site accommodations for visitors to choose from.

Lapita Hotel: Inspired by the South Pacific, Lapita Hotel is a Polynesian-themed resort located within the complex. This luxury hotel provides a tranquil retreat for guests, complete with spacious rooms, fine dining options, a lagoon-style pool, and a spa. Staying at Lapita Hotel offers the convenience of being just a few steps away from the parks, ensuring a seamless and immersive experience.

Resorts in the Vicinity: If you prefer a wider selection of accommodation options, there are several resorts and hotels in close proximity to Dubai Parks and Resorts. From budget-friendly options to five-star luxury properties, visitors can choose from a range of establishments that suit their preferences and budgets. Many of these hotels also offer complimentary shuttle services to the theme parks, making it easy to access the attractions.

Dining and Entertainment:
Dubai Parks and Resorts excels in culinary experiences, with numerous dining options available throughout the complex. From quick bites to fine dining, there is something to cater to every taste and craving. Visitors can enjoy a diverse range of cuisines, including international flavors, Indian delicacies, and traditional Arabic dishes. Additionally, the entertainment scene at Dubai Parks and Resorts is vibrant, with live performances, music festivals, and seasonal events

adding an extra dose of excitement to the overall experience.

Practical Information:

Ticketing and Packages: It is advisable to book tickets in advance to avoid long queues and ensure availability, especially during peak seasons. Dubai Parks and Resorts offers various ticketing options, including single park tickets, multi-park passes, and annual passes for frequent visitors.

Park Timings: The theme parks and attractions within Dubai Parks and Resorts generally operate from late morning until evening. However, it's recommended to check the official website or contact the park for the most up-to-date information regarding opening hours.

Weather Considerations: Dubai experiences a hot desert climate, with temperatures soaring during the summer months. It's essential to stay hydrated, wear sunscreen, and dress appropriately for the weather while visiting the parks. During the cooler months (November to February), the weather is more pleasant and allows for comfortable outdoor exploration.

Family-Friendly Facilities: Dubai Parks and Resorts are designed to be family-friendly, with numerous facilities catering to the needs of young children, including baby changing rooms, stroller rentals, and child-friendly dining options. The parks also provide services for guests with disabilities to ensure an inclusive experience for everyone.

Dubai Parks and Resorts is a remarkable destination that offers a blend of entertainment, adventure, and magical experiences for visitors of all ages. With its diverse array of theme parks, attractions, accommodations, and dining options, it is an ideal place to create lasting memories with family and friends. Whether you are a thrill-seeker, a Bollywood enthusiast, or a Lego lover, Dubai Parks and Resorts will undoubtedly exceed your expectations, leaving you with a sense of wonder and awe in the heart of this vibrant city.

CHAPTER TEN

Events and Festivals

•Dubai Shopping Festival

Dubai, known for its extravagant architecture, luxurious lifestyle, and cultural diversity, offers visitors a plethora of experiences. Among the many attractions in this vibrant city, the Dubai Shopping Festival (DSF) stands out as a flagship event. This annual extravaganza has gained international acclaim and has become a magnet for shopaholics and tourists from around the world. In this comprehensive Dubai travel guide, we will delve into the history, highlights, attractions, and essential tips for experiencing the Dubai Shopping Festival to the fullest.

I. Origins and Evolution of the Dubai Shopping Festival:

The Dubai Shopping Festival made its debut in 1996 and has since transformed into one of the world's largest shopping and entertainment extravaganzas. Initially conceived as a means to boost tourism and promote retail trade, the festival has grown exponentially over the years. From humble beginnings, it has evolved into a month-long celebration of shopping, entertainment, fashion, and culture.

II. Duration and Location:

The Dubai Shopping Festival is held annually, typically spanning a month-long period from late December to early February. The festival takes place in various locations across Dubai, including traditional markets (souks), shopping malls, and outdoor venues. Visitors can explore the festival's offerings throughout the city, creating a vibrant and immersive shopping experience.

III. Highlights and Attractions:

a) Retail Offerings: The Dubai Shopping Festival lives up to its reputation as a shopper's paradise. Visitors can indulge in retail therapy at a wide array of shopping destinations, including iconic malls like The Dubai Mall, Mall of the Emirates, and Ibn Battuta Mall. These venues offer an extensive range of local and international brands, from high-end luxury products to affordable fashion and electronics.

b) Discounts and Promotions: One of the main draws of the Dubai Shopping Festival is the attractive discounts and promotions offered by participating retailers. Bargain hunters can expect significant markdowns on a variety of products, making it an ideal time to splurge on fashion, electronics, jewelry, and more.

c) Fireworks and Light Shows: As night falls, the Dubai Shopping Festival illuminates the sky with breathtaking fireworks displays. Spectacular light shows and multimedia projections on iconic landmarks like the Burj Khalifa and Burj Al Arab create a mesmerizing ambiance, adding to the festival's festive atmosphere.

d) Cultural Events: The festival offers visitors a chance to explore Dubai's rich cultural heritage. Traditional music, dance performances, art exhibitions, and food festivals showcase the city's diverse cultural fabric. Visitors can engage with local traditions, experience Emirati hospitality, and sample regional delicacies.

e) Entertainment and Concerts: The Dubai Shopping Festival goes beyond shopping, providing an eclectic mix of entertainment options. Live concerts featuring internationally renowned artists, dazzling stage shows, street performances, and fashion shows captivate audiences throughout the festival.

IV. Insider Tips for Enjoying the Dubai Shopping Festival:

a) Plan Ahead: Research the festival's schedule, including events, sales, and promotions. Prepare an itinerary to make the most of your time and prioritize the experiences that interest you the most.

b) Budgeting: Set a budget for shopping and entertainment, as the festival can be overwhelming with tempting offers. Prioritize your purchases and resist the temptation to overspend.

c) Dress Comfortably: Dubai's weather during the festival period can be mild to cool. Dress in comfortable attire and wear suitable footwear to navigate the malls and outdoor venues.

d) Public Transportation: Dubai's efficient public transportation system, including the metro and buses, is an excellent way to navigate the city during the festival. It ensures hassle-free travel, especially during peak hours.

e) Local Etiquette: Familiarize yourself with local customs and etiquette to ensure a respectful and enjoyable experience. Dress modestly when visiting religious or cultural sites and be mindful of local traditions and practices.

The Dubai Shopping Festival is a unique event that combines luxury shopping, entertainment, cultural experiences, and an electric atmosphere. From incredible discounts to extravagant entertainment, the festival offers something for everyone. This Dubai travel guide has provided a glimpse into the origins, highlights, and tips for experiencing the Dubai Shopping Festival to its fullest. Embark on a journey to Dubai during the festival, and immerse yourself in an unforgettable shopping extravaganza unlike any other.

- ***Dubai Food Festival***

Dubai, the vibrant city of superlatives, entices travelers from around the world with its luxurious lifestyle, towering skyscrapers, and diverse cultural heritage. Alongside these attractions, Dubai has gained significant recognition as a food lover's paradise. One of the most anticipated events on the city's culinary calendar is the Dubai Food Festival. This annual extravaganza showcases a vibrant tapestry of global flavors, local delicacies, and culinary innovations, making it a must-visit destination for food enthusiasts. In this Dubai travel guide, we will delve into the essence of the Dubai Food Festival, highlighting its key features, unique experiences, and sumptuous offerings.

Origins and Evolution of Dubai Food Festival:
The Dubai Food Festival first emerged in 2014 as a platform to celebrate the city's diverse gastronomic landscape. Over the years, it has grown exponentially, attracting both locals and tourists alike. The festival serves as a melting pot of flavors, where renowned chefs, homegrown talents, and innovative food entrepreneurs come together to showcase their skills and creations.

Duration and Venue :
The Dubai Food Festival typically takes place over several weeks, spanning the month of February and extending into early March. Throughout the festival, various venues across the city come alive with a plethora of food-related activities, pop-up stalls, food trucks, and dining experiences. Some of

the prominent locations include Beach Canteen, Dubai World Trade Centre, and outdoor venues such as La Mer and City Walk.

Signature Events and Highlights :

a) Beach Canteen: As the heart of the festival, Beach Canteen transforms one of Dubai's picturesque beachfronts into a vibrant food paradise. It hosts an array of food stalls representing diverse cuisines, from local Emirati delicacies to international flavors. Visitors can relish tantalizing street food, savor gourmet dishes, and explore unique culinary concepts.

b) Hidden Gems: Dubai's Hidden Gems initiative encourages residents and visitors to explore lesser-known culinary treasures within the city. Participating restaurants offer specially curated menus and exclusive discounts, allowing food enthusiasts to embark on a gastronomic journey off the beaten path.

c) Global Village: During the Dubai Food Festival, Global Village, a cultural extravaganza showcasing the traditions of various countries, incorporates a dedicated section highlighting international cuisine. Visitors can indulge in a diverse range of culinary delights while immersing themselves in the vibrant atmosphere of this multicultural event.

d) Foodie Experiences: Dubai Food Festival offers an array of interactive experiences, such as chef masterclasses, cooking demonstrations, and food photography workshops. These sessions provide participants with insights into the culinary world, enabling them to learn from renowned chefs and industry experts.

e) Food Trucks: Food trucks have become a popular trend in Dubai, and the food festival capitalizes on this by hosting dedicated food truck events. These gatherings bring together a fleet of mobile kitchens, offering a wide range of gourmet street food that satisfies every craving.

Regional and International Flavors :
Dubai's multicultural landscape is beautifully reflected in its diverse culinary offerings. During the festival, visitors can explore flavors from around the world, including Middle Eastern, Indian, Asian, European, and African cuisines. From aromatic shawarmas and succulent kebabs to creamy biryanis and mouthwatering sushi rolls, the food festival presents a gastronomic feast for every palate.

Emirati Cuisine and Local Delights :
The Dubai Food Festival is a perfect opportunity to savor the traditional Emirati cuisine and experience the rich culinary heritage of the region. Visitors can indulge in dishes like Machbous (spiced rice with meat or fish), Harees (slow-cooked wheat and meat), and Luqaimat (sweet dumplings). Local food tours and cultural experiences offer a deeper understanding of Emirati traditions and flavors.

Fine Dining and Michelin-Star Experiences :
Dubai is renowned for its luxurious dining scene, boasting a plethora of fine-dining establishments and Michelin-starred restaurants. During the festival, renowned chefs from around the world collaborate with these prestigious venues to create exclusive menus and culinary experiences. From innovative fusion cuisine to classic dishes reimagined, these dining experiences are a highlight for food connoisseurs.

Dubai's Food Festival encapsulates the city's passion for gastronomy and its dedication to providing a memorable culinary experience. With its diverse range of events, unique offerings, and celebration of global flavors, the festival has become a significant cultural and tourism event. Whether you're a food lover, a culinary enthusiast, or simply looking to explore Dubai's multifaceted dining scene, the Dubai Food Festival promises to take you on an extraordinary culinary journey like no other. Immerse yourself in the tantalizing aromas, diverse tastes, and innovative culinary creations that make this festival an unforgettable experience for all who attend. Plan your visit to Dubai during this gastronomic extravaganza and savor the city's melting pot of flavors.

•*Dubai International Film Festival*

Dubai, known for its architectural wonders and extravagant lifestyle, has also become a hub for the arts and entertainment industry. One of the most prominent cultural events in the region is the Dubai International Film Festival (DIFF). This prestigious festival has been showcasing the best of international and regional cinema since its inception in 2004. In this Dubai travel guide, we will explore the history, significance, and highlights of the Dubai International Film Festival, as well as provide valuable information for visitors interested in attending this spectacular cinematic event.

History and Significance:
The Dubai International Film Festival was established with the aim of promoting cultural exchange, nurturing regional talent, and bridging the gap between Eastern and Western cinema. The inaugural edition took place in 2004, and since then, it has become an annual celebration of film and an essential platform for filmmakers from around the world.

DIFF has played a vital role in establishing Dubai as a global film destination. It has attracted renowned filmmakers, actors, and industry professionals, transforming Dubai into a vibrant cinematic hub. The festival provides a platform for emerging talents and showcases diverse cinematic works, including feature films, documentaries, short films, and experimental projects.

Festival Highlights:
a)Film Screenings: The Dubai International Film Festival presents a rich and diverse selection of films from all genres and countries. The program includes world premieres, regional premieres, and

special screenings of highly anticipated movies. Visitors have the opportunity to watch exceptional films that are not easily accessible elsewhere.

b) Red Carpet Glamour: DIFF is known for its glitz and glamour. Celebrities from the film industry, including Hollywood and Arab stars, grace the red carpet and attend gala screenings. The festival provides a unique chance for film enthusiasts to witness their favorite actors and directors up close.

c) Industry Events: The festival hosts a range of workshops, panel discussions, and masterclasses led by industry experts. These events offer invaluable insights into various aspects of filmmaking, acting, and the business of cinema. It serves as an excellent platform for networking and knowledge exchange.

d) Awards: DIFF recognizes outstanding talent through its competitive award categories, including Best Film, Best Director, and Best Actor/Actress. The awards celebrate cinematic excellence and contribute to the global recognition of filmmakers.

Venue and Dates:
The Dubai International Film Festival usually takes place in December, attracting visitors from around the globe. The festival primarily takes place at the

state-of-the-art Madinat Jumeirah complex, which offers world-class facilities for screenings, events, and networking. Located near the iconic Burj Al Arab, Madinat Jumeirah provides a stunning backdrop for the festival.

Planning Your Visit:

a) Tickets: Attendees can purchase tickets for film screenings and special events through the official Dubai International Film Festival website or designated ticketing outlets. Prices may vary depending on the category and type of .

b) Accommodation: Dubai offers a wide range of accommodation options to suit every budget. From luxurious hotels near the festival venue to more affordable options in different areas of the city, visitors can find accommodation that suits their preferences and requirements.

c) Transportation: Dubai has a well-connected transportation system, including taxis, ride-hailing services, and a metro network. Visitors can easily navigate the city to reach the festival venue and explore other attractions during their stay.

d) Dress Code and Etiquette: While attending film screenings and red carpet events, it is advisable to dress formally or semi-formally. Visitors are expected to respect local customs and cultural sensitivities during their time in Dubai.

Beyond the Festival:
Dubai offers a multitude of attractions beyond the film festival. Visitors can explore iconic landmarks such as the Burj Khalifa, Palm Jumeirah, and Dubai Mall. The city also boasts exquisite dining options, luxury shopping experiences, and vibrant nightlife. Additionally, Dubai's unique blend of traditional and modern architecture provides a fascinating backdrop for photography enthusiasts.

The Dubai International Film Festival has successfully established itself as a premier cinematic event in the Middle East. By promoting cultural exchange and showcasing the best of international and regional cinema, DIFF has contributed to the growth of Dubai's film industry and elevated its status as a global cultural destination. Attending this prestigious festival is not only an opportunity to experience exceptional films but also a chance to immerse oneself in the glamour and charm of Dubai's vibrant entertainment scene.

• Eid Al-Fitr and Eid Al-Adha

Dubai, the vibrant and cosmopolitan city in the United Arab Emirates, offers a rich cultural tapestry with a fusion of tradition and modernity. One of the best times to experience Dubai's unique cultural heritage is during the celebrations of Eid Al-Fitr and Eid Al-Adha. These two Islamic festivals hold immense significance for Muslims worldwide and provide a glimpse into Dubai's religious customs, festivities, and warm hospitality. In this comprehensive travel guide, we will explore the essence of Eid Al-Fitr and Eid Al-Adha in Dubai, highlighting the traditions, activities, and attractions that visitors can enjoy during these joyous occasions.

I. Eid Al-Fitr: The Festival of Breaking the Fast

Eid Al-Fitr marks the end of the holy month of Ramadan, a period of fasting and spiritual reflection for Muslims. In Dubai, the festival is celebrated with great enthusiasm and fervor, bringing together locals and visitors in a joyful atmosphere. Here's what you need to know about experiencing Eid Al-Fitr in Dubai:

Preparations and Traditions :

Observing the final days of Ramadan: Witness the dedication and devotion of Muslims as they engage in prayer, recitation of the Quran, and acts of charity.
Shopping for Eid: Explore the bustling markets and shopping malls, such as the Dubai Mall and Mall of the Emirates, where you can find traditional attire, accessories, and gifts.
Henna art: Embrace the local customs by adorning your hands with intricate henna designs, a popular tradition during Eid festivities.
Prayers and Sermons (200 words):

Attend the Eid prayers at prominent mosques in Dubai, such as the Jumeirah Mosque or the Dubai Mosque, to witness the unity and spirituality of the local community.
Listen to inspiring sermons delivered by respected Islamic scholars, emphasizing the values of gratitude, forgiveness, and community harmony.
Festive Delights and Cuisine (200 words):

Indulge in mouthwatering traditional Emirati dishes, including aromatic biryanis, flavorful kebabs, and delectable sweets like baklava and luqaimat.

Visit the local food markets, such as the Dubai Spice Souk and the Deira Fish Market, to experience the vibrant flavors and scents of the Middle East.

Family Bonding and Entertainment (250 words):

Join in the joyous gatherings with families and friends, where traditional dances, music, and cultural performances add to the festive ambiance.

Take part in fun activities like camel rides, falconry shows, and traditional games, creating lasting memories of Eid Al-Fitr in Dubai.

Visit Dubai's amusement parks, such as IMG Worlds of Adventure or Dubai Parks and Resorts, which offer special Eid promotions and entertainment for families.

II. Eid Al-Adha: The Festival of Sacrifice

Eid Al-Adha commemorates the willingness of Prophet Ibrahim to sacrifice his son as an act of obedience to God. This festival showcases the spirit of sacrifice, generosity, and community. In Dubai, visitors can experience the essence of Eid Al-Adha through various activities and traditions:

Prayer and Reflection :

Attend the Eid Al-Adha prayers at iconic landmarks like the Sheikh Zayed Grand Mosque or the Dubai World Trade Centre, witnessing the congregational prayers and sermons.
Reflect on the significance of sacrifice and participate in communal acts of charity, such as donating food, clothes, or money to those in need.

Livestock Markets and Animal Welfare :

Explore Dubai's livestock markets, such as the Al Qusais Livestock Market, where you can witness the purchase and preparation of sacrificial animals.
Understand the importance of animal welfare during Eid Al-Adha by visiting animal shelters or farms that prioritize ethical treatment.

Festive Feasts and Hospitality :

Enjoy traditional dishes like mandi, harees, and ouzi, which are prepared using the meat from sacrificial animals, and savor the warm hospitality extended by local Emirati families.

Experience the famous "Eidiyah," where children and young adults receive monetary gifts from elders as a gesture of love and blessings.

Cultural Experiences and Entertainment (250 words):

Immerse yourself in the rich Emirati heritage and Bedouin traditions through cultural performances, including folk dances, music, and storytelling.

Witness thrilling camel races, falconry displays, and equestrian shows, showcasing the region's longstanding cultural practices.

Visit historical sites like the Dubai Museum, Sheikh Saeed Al Maktoum House, and Al Fahidi Historic District to learn about Dubai's past and its role in preserving cultural heritage.

Celebrating Eid Al-Fitr and Eid Al-Adha in Dubai offers a unique opportunity to witness the vibrant traditions, religious customs, and warm hospitality of the local Emirati community. Whether you choose to participate in the prayers, indulge in traditional cuisine, or engage in cultural activities, these festivals provide an unforgettable experience that embodies the spirit of unity, generosity, and togetherness. As you explore Dubai during these festive seasons, remember to embrace the local customs, respect the religious significance, and enjoy the rich cultural tapestry that this incredible city has to offer.

- **Dubai World Cup**

Dubai, known for its opulence and grandeur, offers a myriad of unforgettable experiences for travelers. Among its remarkable events, the Dubai World Cup stands out as a highlight on the city's social and sporting calendar. This prestigious horse racing extravaganza attracts enthusiasts from around the world, combining thrilling races with lavish entertainment and luxurious amenities. In this Dubai travel guide, we delve into the captivating world of the Dubai World Cup, exploring its history, the venue, the races, and the overall experience it offers.

History and Significance:
The Dubai World Cup, inaugurated in 1996, quickly established itself as one of the most important horse racing events globally. It was the visionary project of His Highness Sheikh Mohammed bin Rashid Al Maktoum, Vice President and Prime

Minister of the UAE and Ruler of Dubai. This event marked a significant milestone in Dubai's journey towards becoming a global hub for sports, entertainment, and tourism.

Venue: Meydan Racecourse - A Spectacular Oasis:
The Dubai World Cup is hosted at the magnificent Meydan Racecourse, a world-class facility designed to impress even the most discerning visitors. Spanning over 7.5 million square feet, the racecourse boasts state-of-the-art amenities, including a stunning grandstand, luxurious hospitality suites, and a sprawling apron that can accommodate over 60,000 spectators.

The Races: A Showcase of Equine Excellence:
The Dubai World Cup offers an exceptional lineup of races, featuring some of the finest thoroughbred horses from around the globe. The main event, the Dubai World Cup race itself, carries a staggering prize purse of $12 million, making it the richest horse race in the world. Other notable races during the day include the Dubai Sheema Classic, Dubai Turf, and Dubai Golden Shaheen, each attracting top-class competitors.

The Dubai World Cup Experience:

a. Extravagant Hospitality: Spectators can indulge in a range of hospitality options, including private suites, lounges, and exclusive dining experiences. From gourmet cuisine to impeccable service, every detail is meticulously designed to offer a truly memorable experience.

b. Fashion and Glamour: The Dubai World Cup is not just about horse racing; it is a fashion showcase where attendees flaunt their stylish attire and vie for the coveted Best Dressed title. The event sets the stage for glamorous fashion parades, adding an extra layer of excitement and elegance.

c. Entertainment and Performances: The Dubai World Cup goes beyond racing, providing a variety of entertainment options to cater to diverse tastes. Spectacular live performances by world-renowned artists, stunning firework displays, and captivating cultural shows contribute to the electric atmosphere that permeates the event.

d. Betting and Gaming: For those who wish to try their luck, the Dubai World Cup offers various betting options. From traditional bookmakers to modern digital platforms, visitors can place wagers on their favorite horses and races, adding an element of thrill and anticipation.

Beyond the Racecourse: Exploring Dubai's Extravagance:
While the Dubai World Cup is undeniably the centerpiece of this grand event, visitors can also explore Dubai's iconic attractions and luxurious offerings. From indulging in high-end shopping at the Dubai Mall to experiencing the architectural marvels of Burj Khalifa and Palm Jumeirah, Dubai promises a wealth of experiences to complement the racing excitement.

Sustainability and Social Impact:
The Dubai World Cup takes great strides in incorporating sustainability initiatives and raising awareness about social causes. From implementing eco-friendly practices at the racecourse to supporting local charities and community projects, the event contributes positively to Dubai's sustainable development goals.

The Dubai World Cup is a celebration of luxury, sport, and entertainment that epitomizes the city's remarkable spirit. Whether you are a passionate horse racing enthusiast or simply seeking an extraordinary experience, this event offers an unparalleled blend of world-class racing, opulent hospitality, and unforgettable moments. As you explore Dubai, make sure to mark the Dubai World Cup on your calendar for an unforgettable journey into the heart of Arabian hospitality and glamour.

• *New Year's Celebrations*

Dubai, the dazzling city of the United Arab Emirates, is renowned for its opulent lifestyle, breathtaking architecture, and extravagant events. When it comes to New Year's celebrations, Dubai sets the bar high, offering visitors a truly unforgettable experience. From stunning fireworks displays to world-class entertainment, Dubai transforms into a magical wonderland during this festive time. In this comprehensive travel guide, we will explore the various highlights and activities that make Dubai an exceptional destination to welcome the New Year.

Festive Atmosphere and Preparations

Dubai embraces the New Year with an unparalleled enthusiasm that can be felt throughout the city. As the year draws to a close, preparations begin in earnest. The streets, shopping malls, and iconic landmarks are adorned with festive decorations, creating a vibrant and joyful ambiance. The city's renowned hospitality industry takes center stage, offering a wide range of luxurious accommodations and special packages for visitors seeking to celebrate in style.

Spectacular Fireworks Displays
One of the most highly anticipated events in Dubai during New Year's Eve is the spectacular fireworks display. The city's skyline transforms into a kaleidoscope of colors as mesmerizing pyrotechnic shows take place at various iconic locations. The Burj Khalifa, the world's tallest building, serves as the centerpiece for the fireworks extravaganza, captivating audiences with its synchronized display. Other popular locations include the Palm Jumeirah, Atlantis, The Palm, and Burj Al Arab, where fireworks illuminate the night sky, creating an enchanting spectacle that attracts millions of visitors.

Dhow Cruise Experience
For a unique New Year's celebration, embark on a traditional dhow cruise along Dubai Creek or Dubai Marina. These enchanting wooden boats offer a delightful experience, combining a scenic cruise with live entertainment and a sumptuous dinner. Guests can revel in the stunning views of the city's

skyline while enjoying traditional music, dance performances, and a delectable feast. As the clock strikes midnight, witness the fireworks from a different perspective, creating memories that will last a lifetime.

Festive Dining and Entertainment
Dubai's renowned culinary scene comes alive during New Year's celebrations, with a plethora of dining options to suit every palate. The city's world-class restaurants, hotels, and resorts offer special menus and themed evenings, providing a gastronomic journey of flavors from around the world. From elegant fine dining establishments to vibrant street food markets, visitors can indulge in an array of cuisines and culinary experiences.

Moreover, Dubai hosts a lineup of spectacular live performances and entertainment shows during this time. From concerts by international artists to dazzling stage productions, there is no shortage of entertainment options for visitors to enjoy. The city's entertainment venues and nightlife hotspots come alive with energy, making it an ideal destination for those looking to party into the early hours of the morning.

Shopping Extravaganza

Dubai's reputation as a shopper's paradise is amplified during New Year's celebrations. The city's world-class shopping malls and traditional souks offer incredible discounts and promotions, enticing visitors with unbeatable deals. The Dubai Shopping Festival, held from December to January, coincides with the New Year celebrations, making it an ideal time to shop for luxury brands, electronics, fashion, and local handicrafts. Additionally, various entertainment activities, live performances, and fireworks displays are organized at shopping destinations, creating a festive and vibrant atmosphere for shoppers.

Dubai's New Year's celebrations are truly a sight to behold, offering an unmatched combination of luxury, entertainment, and cultural experiences. From the dazzling fireworks displays illuminating the city's skyline to the vibrant festivities and world-class entertainment, Dubai promises a memorable start to the New Year. Whether you choose to indulge in a lavish dining experience, embark on a traditional dhow cruise, or immerse yourself in the city's vibrant nightlife, Dubai's celebrations are sure to leave you awe-inspired. Plan your trip in advance, secure your accommodations, and get ready to ring in the New

Year in the most extravagant and unforgettable way possible in the magnificent city of Dubai.

CHAPTER ELEVEN

Practical Tips and Resources

•*Important Phone Numbers*

Dubai, a captivating city that seamlessly blends ancient traditions with modern luxuries, has become one of the most sought-after travel destinations in the world. To ensure a smooth and hassle-free experience during your visit to Dubai, it is essential to have access to important phone numbers. In this comprehensive travel guide, we will provide you with a curated list of crucial phone numbers in Dubai, ranging from emergency services to transportation, accommodation, and other essential services. Equipped with these numbers, you can confidently explore the city and address any situation that may arise.

Emergency Services

In any travel destination, having access to emergency services is of paramount importance. In

Dubai, the following phone numbers are crucial for emergency situations:

Police: Dial 999 for immediate police assistance. The Dubai Police Force is renowned for its efficiency and professionalism.

Ambulance: Dial 998 to request an ambulance in case of a medical emergency. Trained professionals will promptly respond to your call and provide necessary medical aid.

Fire Department: Dial 997 to reach the Dubai Civil Defence in case of a fire or other related emergencies.

Healthcare Services

When traveling, it is vital to be aware of healthcare services available in the destination. In Dubai, the following phone numbers will help you access medical assistance:

Dubai Health Authority (DHA) Helpline: Dial 800-DHA (800-342) for general inquiries and information about healthcare facilities, clinics, and hospitals in Dubai.

Rashid Hospital: +971 4 219 2000. A prominent public hospital in Dubai that offers a wide range of medical services.

American Hospital Dubai: +971 4 377 5500. A renowned private hospital catering to international standards of healthcare.

Aster Hospital: +971 4 440 0500. A leading medical institution providing comprehensive healthcare services to residents and visitors.

Transportation Services (500 words)

Dubai offers various modes of transportation to navigate the city efficiently. The following phone numbers will assist you in accessing transportation services:

Dubai Taxi Corporation: Dial 04-2080808 to book a taxi or inquire about taxi services in Dubai. Taxis are readily available and are a convenient mode of transportation within the city.

Dubai Metro: Dial 800 90 90 or visit www.rta.ae for information on Dubai's metro system, including stations, timings, and fares. The metro is an efficient way to travel across different areas of Dubai.

Dubai Bus Service: Dial 800-9090 for information about Dubai's bus routes, schedules, and fares. The bus service covers a wide network, connecting various neighborhoods and attractions.

Dubai Tram: Dial 800 90 90 or visit www.rta.ae for information on Dubai's tram system, including routes, timings, and fares. The tram offers easy access to popular destinations along the city's coastline.

Dubai International Airport: Dial +971 4 224 5555 for general inquiries, flight information, and assistance at Dubai's international airport, one of the busiest airports in the world.

Tourist Information
For comprehensive information about Dubai's attractions, events, and services, the following phone numbers will be helpful:
Department of Tourism and Commerce Marketing (DTCM): Dial +971 600 55 5559 for general inquiries and tourist information. The DTCM provides valuable insights into Dubai's attractions, cultural events, and local regulations.
Dubai Tourism Helpline: Dial 600 55 5559 for 24/7 tourist assistance. The helpline can assist with queries regarding visas, hotel bookings, and general tourist information.
Dubai Visitor Center: Dial 800 9090 for visitor information, maps, brochures, and guidance on exploring Dubai's diverse offerings.

Accommodation Services
Dubai boasts a wide range of hotels and accommodations to suit every budget. The following phone numbers will help you make inquiries and reservations:
Hotel Reception: Contact the front desk of your chosen hotel directly for any queries, reservations, or assistance during your stay.

Booking Platforms: Utilize online booking platforms such as Booking.com, Expedia, or Airbnb to find and book accommodations that suit your preferences and budget.

Dubai's vibrant and cosmopolitan atmosphere attracts millions of visitors each year. By equipping yourself with these essential phone numbers, you can ensure a safe and memorable experience in this remarkable city. Remember to store these numbers in your phone or keep them easily accessible throughout your trip. Additionally, it is always recommended to have travel insurance that covers emergency situations and medical expenses during your visit. Embrace the beauty of Dubai, explore its iconic landmarks, indulge in its rich culture, and rest assured knowing you have the necessary resources at your fingertips to navigate any situation that may arise.

• *Internet and Communication*

Dubai, the gleaming jewel of the United Arab Emirates, is known for its luxurious lifestyle, ultramodern architecture, and thriving business environment. As a global hub for tourism and commerce, Dubai recognizes the importance of efficient internet and communication services to cater to the needs of its residents and visitors. In this comprehensive travel guide, we will delve into the state of internet and communication in Dubai, exploring the evolution of technology, infrastructure, and services over the years.

Telecommunications Infrastructure:
Dubai boasts a robust and advanced telecommunications infrastructure that supports the growing demand for high-speed internet and reliable communication services. The backbone of this infrastructure is the Dubai Fiber Optic Network, which spans across the city, providing seamless connectivity and high bandwidth. This extensive network ensures fast and reliable internet access throughout Dubai, whether you are in a hotel, restaurant, shopping mall, or public space.

Internet Connectivity:
Dubai offers widespread internet connectivity options to cater to the diverse needs of its residents and visitors. Most hotels, resorts, and serviced

apartments provide complimentary high-speed Wi-Fi access to guests, ensuring they stay connected throughout their stay. Additionally, numerous public spaces, including parks, beaches, and transportation hubs, offer free Wi-Fi hotspots, allowing travelers to access the internet on the go.

For those seeking a more dedicated and secure internet connection, various internet service providers (ISPs) in Dubai offer a range of plans tailored to different requirements. Du and Etisalat are the two major ISPs in the city, providing reliable internet services to residential and commercial users. Whether you need internet access for work, leisure, or staying connected with loved ones back home, Dubai offers a wide array of options to suit your needs.

Mobile Communication:
Dubai has a well-established mobile communication infrastructure, ensuring seamless connectivity for both local and international visitors. The city operates on the Global System for Mobile Communications (GSM) standard, enabling compatibility with most international mobile networks. Visitors can choose to use their existing mobile phones by activating international roaming

or purchase local SIM cards for better affordability and convenience.

Du and Etisalat, the primary telecom operators in Dubai, offer a range of prepaid and postpaid mobile plans catering to different communication needs. These plans often include generous data allowances, international calling options, and additional services such as voicemail and call forwarding. Both operators have widespread coverage across the city, including remote areas and popular tourist destinations, ensuring uninterrupted communication for travelers.

Internet and Communication Regulations:
While Dubai embraces technological advancements, it is important to note that the city has certain regulations regarding internet and communication usage. Dubai's authorities place restrictions on accessing certain websites and content that are deemed inappropriate or offensive according to local laws and customs. Platforms and services such as Voice over Internet Protocol (VoIP) applications may also be limited or blocked.

To ensure a smooth and hassle-free experience, visitors are advised to respect local regulations and use the internet and communication services responsibly. It is recommended to familiarize yourself with the local laws and guidelines to avoid any inconvenience during your stay in Dubai.

Internet Cafes and Business Centers:
For travelers who do not have their own devices or require access to computers and other business services, Dubai offers a multitude of internet cafes and business centers. These establishments provide computer terminals with internet access, printing facilities, scanning services, and more. Internet cafes are often conveniently located in popular tourist areas, making it easy to find a place to check emails, surf the web, or complete essential tasks.

Emerging Technologies:
Dubai is at the forefront of embracing emerging technologies that further enhance internet and communication experiences. The city is actively investing in the development of 5G infrastructure, aiming to provide ultra-fast and reliable internet connectivity to residents and visitors. As 5G technology continues to roll out, Dubai will be poised to offer enhanced mobile communication, seamless streaming, and innovative digital experiences.

Furthermore, Dubai has been a pioneer in adopting smart city initiatives, integrating technology into various aspects of daily life. From smart transportation systems to IoT-enabled services, Dubai's vision of becoming a smart city enhances the overall internet and communication landscape, ensuring a connected and convenient experience for all.

Dubai's commitment to providing excellent internet and communication services has undoubtedly played a significant role in its reputation as a global destination for tourism and business. With its advanced telecommunications infrastructure, widespread connectivity options, and ongoing technological advancements, Dubai ensures that residents and visitors can stay connected, productive, and entertained throughout their stay. As you embark on your journey to this remarkable city, embrace the seamless internet and communication services Dubai has to offer, and enjoy a truly connected experience.

• Health and Safety

Dubai, a vibrant city in the United Arab Emirates (UAE), has become a top tourist destination known for its modern architecture, luxury shopping, and rich cultural experiences. As you embark on your journey to this captivating city, it is essential to familiarize yourself with the health and safety guidelines to ensure a pleasant and worry-free visit. This comprehensive guide aims to provide you with valuable insights and practical tips to navigate Dubai's health and safety landscape, covering various aspects such as healthcare facilities, food and water safety, transportation safety, weather considerations, and emergency services.

Healthcare Facilities and Services:

Dubai boasts a well-developed healthcare infrastructure that meets international standards. The city has a range of public and private hospitals, clinics, and medical centers equipped with state-of-the-art facilities and highly trained medical professionals. Some renowned hospitals in Dubai include the Dubai Hospital, Rashid Hospital, and American Hospital Dubai. Moreover, Dubai Healthcare City, a dedicated healthcare free zone, offers specialized medical services in various fields.

It is crucial to have comprehensive travel insurance that covers medical emergencies before your trip to Dubai. In case of any health concerns, contact the Dubai Health Authority (DHA) hotline or visit the nearest healthcare facility. Keep in mind that medical services in Dubai can be expensive, so it is advisable to have adequate insurance coverage.

Food and Water Safety:
Dubai is known for its diverse culinary scene, offering a plethora of dining options ranging from street food to world-class restaurants. While the majority of food establishments adhere to strict hygiene standards, it is essential to exercise caution to avoid any potential health risks.

a. Water Safety: Tap water in Dubai is generally considered safe for drinking, as it undergoes a rigorous desalination process. However, some visitors prefer to consume bottled water to be on the safer side. Ensure that the seal on the water bottle is intact before purchasing it.

b. Food Hygiene: When dining out, choose reputable restaurants and eateries that display high standards of cleanliness. Check for proper food handling and storage practices. It is advisable to avoid consuming raw or undercooked food, especially seafood, to prevent the risk of foodborne illnesses. Additionally, remember to wash your hands regularly before meals or carry a hand sanitizer for convenience.

Transportation Safety:
Dubai provides various transportation options, including taxis, buses, the Dubai Metro, and ride-hailing services like Uber and Careem. To ensure your safety while getting around the city, consider the following:

a. Taxis: Use only official taxis with a visible meter and make sure the driver starts the meter upon commencing the journey. Taxis in Dubai are generally safe and well-regulated.

b. Public Transportation: The Dubai Metro and buses are efficient and well-maintained modes of transportation. Follow the designated safety guidelines, such as keeping personal belongings secure and following any instructions or announcements.

c. Ride-Hailing Services: Services like Uber and Careem are widely available in Dubai. Ensure that the driver and vehicle details match the information provided in the app before getting into the car.

Weather Considerations:
Dubai experiences a desert climate characterized by high temperatures and low humidity. To stay safe and comfortable during your visit, consider the following weather-related precautions:

a. Sun Protection: The sun can be intense in Dubai, so it is crucial to protect yourself from excessive sun exposure. Use sunscreen with a high SPF, wear sunglasses, a wide-brimmed hat, and lightweight, breathable clothing.

b. Heat and Hydration: Stay hydrated by drinking plenty of water throughout the day, especially during hot weather. Consider carrying a water bottle with you to ensure you have access to water at all times.

c. Sandstorms: Occasionally, Dubai experiences sandstorms or dusty conditions. During such times, it is advisable to stay indoors, close windows and doors, and avoid unnecessary exposure to the dusty environment.

Emergency Services:
In case of any emergencies, Dubai provides a robust emergency response system. The emergency hotline

number in Dubai is 999. This number can be dialed for immediate assistance in case of accidents, medical emergencies, or any other urgent situations. Ensure that you have this number saved in your phone for quick access.

Dubai, with its blend of modernity and cultural heritage, offers a remarkable travel experience. By familiarizing yourself with the health and safety guidelines outlined in this comprehensive guide, you can ensure a smooth and secure visit to this captivating city. From accessing quality healthcare facilities to practicing food and water safety, and navigating transportation options, these guidelines will help you make informed decisions and enjoy your time in Dubai to the fullest. Remember, prioritizing your health and safety will contribute to an unforgettable and worry-free travel experience in Dubai.

•*Etiquette and Cultural Considerations*

Dubai, a thriving cosmopolitan city in the United Arab Emirates, has become a popular tourist destination known for its stunning architecture, luxury shopping, and vibrant cultural experiences. As a visitor to Dubai, it is essential to familiarize yourself with the local customs, etiquette, and cultural considerations to ensure a respectful and enjoyable stay. This comprehensive travel guide aims to provide you with insights into the etiquette and cultural nuances of Dubai, allowing you to navigate the city with confidence and appreciation for its rich heritage.

Islamic Culture and Religion:
Dubai is deeply rooted in Islamic culture and religion, and it is important to respect and acknowledge these aspects during your visit. Some key considerations include:

a. Dress Code: While Dubai is a modern city, modesty in dressing is highly valued, especially in public areas. Both men and women should avoid wearing revealing or tight-fitting clothing. Women are advised to cover their shoulders and knees, and it is customary for them to wear a headscarf when visiting religious sites.

b. Respect for Ramadan: If your visit coincides with the holy month of Ramadan, it is important to be aware of the customs observed during this time. It is respectful to refrain from eating, drinking, or smoking in public places during daylight hours. Many restaurants and cafes remain closed until sunset, but hotels usually offer designated dining areas for non-Muslims.

c. Religious Sites: Dubai is home to magnificent mosques, such as the Jumeirah Mosque. Non-Muslims are generally welcome to visit these places of worship, but it is crucial to dress modestly and remove shoes before entering. Additionally, be mindful of the prayer times and avoid visiting during these periods.

Greeting and Communication:
Dubai is a multicultural city, and people from different backgrounds reside and work here. However, there are certain norms and customs to follow when interacting with locals:

a. Greetings: Traditional greetings in Dubai involve a gentle handshake and the Arabic phrase "As-salamu alaykum" (peace be upon you). Men should wait for women to initiate a handshake, as some may prefer not to engage in physical contact. It is also polite to address people by their title and surname, using "Mr." or "Ms." until given permission to use their first name.

b. Language: Arabic is the official language of Dubai, but English is widely spoken and understood. It is recommended to learn a few common Arabic phrases, such as "thank you" (shukran) and "please" (min fadlik), to demonstrate respect for the local culture.

c. Nonverbal Communication: Nonverbal cues play a significant role in communication. Maintaining eye contact during conversations shows attentiveness and respect. Public displays of affection should be avoided, as they are considered inappropriate in the local culture.

Social Etiquette:
Understanding the social customs in Dubai will help you navigate social situations with ease:
a. Hospitality: Emiratis are known for their warm hospitality, and it is common to be invited into homes for meals or traditional gatherings. Accepting these invitations is a wonderful opportunity to experience Emirati culture firsthand. When invited, it is polite to bring a small gift, such as chocolates or flowers, as a token of appreciation.

b. Dining Etiquette: When dining with Emiratis, it is customary to eat with your right hand, as the left hand is considered unclean. Remember to remove your shoes when entering someone's home, and wait to be seated or instructed where to sit. It is polite to accept second helpings, as it demonstrates appreciation for the host's hospitality.

c. Tipping: Tipping is not mandatory in Dubai, as a service charge is often included in bills at hotels and restaurants. However, if you receive exceptional service, it is customary to leave a small tip to show your gratitude.

Cultural Sensitivities:
Respecting local customs and sensitivities is crucial during your stay in Dubai:
a. Alcohol Consumption: While alcohol is served in licensed establishments such as hotels and bars, it is important to remember that public intoxication is frowned upon. It is also illegal to consume alcohol in public places, so always drink responsibly and within designated areas.

b. Photography: Dubai offers numerous picturesque locations, but it is advisable to ask for permission before photographing individuals, especially women, as some may prefer not to be photographed. Additionally, avoid taking pictures of government buildings or military installations, as it is prohibited.

c. Cultural Events and Festivals: Dubai hosts a variety of cultural events and festivals throughout the year, such as the Dubai Shopping Festival and Dubai Food Festival. Attending these events provides an excellent opportunity to immerse yourself in the local culture and traditions.

As you embark on your journey to Dubai, understanding the etiquette and cultural considerations will greatly enhance your experience and foster positive interactions with locals. Embracing the customs and traditions of this vibrant city will not only demonstrate your respect for the local culture but also allow you to connect with the heart and soul of Dubai. By following the guidelines outlined in this travel guide, you are well-equipped to make the most of your visit while leaving a positive and lasting impression on the people you meet along the way. Safe travels!

CHAPTER TWELVE

Conclusion

In conclusion, Dubai is a truly extraordinary destination that offers a unique blend of tradition and modernity, making it an ideal choice for travelers seeking an unforgettable experience. Throughout this comprehensive travel guide, we have explored the various facets of this magnificent city, from its iconic landmarks to its rich cultural heritage, from its luxurious shopping malls to its serene desert landscapes.

Dubai's architectural marvels, such as the Burj Khalifa, Palm Jumeirah, and Dubai Marina, showcase the city's ambition and determination to push boundaries. These landmarks not only captivate visitors with their grandeur but also offer unparalleled views and experiences that leave a lasting impression. The city's skyline, adorned with glittering skyscrapers and innovative structures, is a testament to Dubai's pursuit of excellence in architecture and urban planning.

Beyond its architectural prowess, Dubai takes pride in its diverse and multicultural society. With a melting pot of nationalities and cultures, the city embraces diversity, creating a vibrant and harmonious atmosphere. Visitors can immerse themselves in the local culture by exploring traditional souks, trying authentic Emirati cuisine, or witnessing traditional performances such as Tanoura dances and falconry shows. Dubai's commitment to preserving its heritage is evident in the beautifully restored Al Fahidi Historic District, where visitors can stroll through its narrow lanes, visit museums, and gain insight into Dubai's past.

For those seeking retail therapy, Dubai's reputation as a shopping paradise is well-deserved. From world-class luxury brands to traditional markets, the city offers an unmatched shopping experience. The Dubai Mall, Mall of the Emirates, and Ibn Battuta Mall are just a few of the sprawling shopping complexes that cater to all tastes and budgets. Dubai's annual shopping festivals attract millions of visitors with their incredible discounts, entertainment events, and raffle draws, making it a shopper's dream come true.

While Dubai may be synonymous with opulence and luxury, the city also provides ample opportunities for relaxation and rejuvenation. Its pristine beaches, such as Jumeirah Beach and Kite

Beach, offer a tranquil escape from the bustling city. Visitors can indulge in water sports, sunbathe on the golden sands, or enjoy a leisurely stroll along the waterfront promenades. Additionally, Dubai boasts an impressive selection of world-class spas and wellness retreats, providing a haven for those seeking serenity and pampering.

Beyond the city's boundaries lies the vast Arabian Desert, where visitors can experience the timeless beauty of the dunes and engage in thrilling activities such as dune bashing, camel riding, and sandboarding. Desert safaris offer a glimpse into Bedouin culture, allowing visitors to savor traditional Arabic cuisine, watch captivating performances, and sleep under a blanket of stars in luxurious desert camps.

Furthermore, Dubai's commitment to hosting international events and exhibitions has firmly established it as a global hub for business and leisure. The city's state-of-the-art convention centers, such as the Dubai World Trade Centre, attract business travelers from around the world, while events like the Dubai Expo showcase innovation, sustainability, and cultural exchange on a grand scale. These initiatives reinforce Dubai's position as a forward-thinking and dynamic city, constantly striving to shape the future.

It is important to note that Dubai's meteoric rise as a global tourist destination would not have been possible without the Emirate's visionary leadership and relentless pursuit of excellence. The government's commitment to developing world-class infrastructure, ensuring safety and security, and promoting sustainability has played a pivotal role in Dubai's success. The city's efficient public transportation system, including the Dubai Metro and extensive network of buses and taxis, makes getting around convenient and hassle-free.

In conclusion, Dubai offers a multitude of experiences that cater to every traveler's preferences. Whether you are seeking adventure, luxury, culture, or relaxation, this vibrant city has something for everyone. From the awe-inspiring architectural wonders to the warm hospitality of its people, Dubai never fails to leave a lasting impression. As you embark on your journey to this extraordinary destination, prepare to be captivated by its allure and create memories that will last a lifetime.